THE POETRY OF LOVE

Erato, Muse of Lyric Poetry
From a painting by Charles Meynier (1763-1832)

Front cover and title page vignettes by Henri Matisse

THE POETRY OF LOVE

AN ECLECTIC ANTHOLOGY

Selected, translated, and adapted
by
John E. Tidball

BISHOPSTON EDITIONS

Copyright © 2025 by John E. Tidball

Bishopston Editions, Bristol, England

All rights reserved

ISBN 978-1-9191772-4-3

CONTENTS

Foreword   13

Pierre de Ronsard (1524 – 1585)
Ode to Cassandra   15
Sonnet for Helen   16

Nicholas Breton (1542 - 1626)
Fair and True   17

Edmund Spenser (c.1552-1599)
Ice and Fire   18
One day I wrote her name…   19

Sir Philip Sidney (1554-86)
My true love hath my heart…   20

Michael Drayton (1563-1631)
Since there's no help…   21

William Shakespeare (1564 - 1616)
Sonnet 18   22
Sonnet 116   23
Sonnet 130   24
Sonnet 147   25

Christopher Marlowe (1564 – 1593)
The Passionate Shepherd to his Love   26
Who Ever Loved, That Loved Not at First Sight?   27

Thomas Campion (c.1567-1619
Amaryllis   28

Ben Jonson (1572 - 1637)
Song to Celia – I : *Come, my Celia, let us prove…*   29
Song to Celia – II : *Drink to me only with thine eyes…*   30

John Wilbye (1574 – 1638)
Love not me for comely grace…   31

John Fletcher (1579 - 1625)
Take, oh, take those lips away…   32

CONTENTS

Thomas Ford (1580—1648)
There is a lady sweet and kind…   33

Robert Herrick (1591-1674)
To Virgins, to make much of Time   34
Sweet Disorder   35

George Herbert (1593 – 1633)
Love bade me welcome…   36

Sir John Suckling (1609 – 1641)
I prithee send me back my heart…   37

Anne Bradstreet (1612 – 1672)
To My Dear and Loving Husband   38

Richard Lovelace (1617 – 1657)
Tell me not, Sweet, I am unkind…   39

John Dryden (1631 - 1700)
Hidden Flame   40

John Wilmot (1647 – 1680)
Love and Life   41

Samuel Johnson (1709 – 1784)
Evening Ode   42
The Winter's Walk   43
Summer   44
To Stella   45

Johann Wolfgang von Goethe (1749-1832)
Would You Were Here!   46
Welcome and Farewell   47

Leonard McNally (1752 –1820)
The Lass of Richmond Hill   48

William Blake (1757 – 1827)
The Garden of Love   49
My Pretty Rose Tree   50

CONTENTS

Robert Burns (1759-1796)
A Red, Red Rose ... 51
The Parting Kiss ... 52

Amelia Opie (1769 – 1853)
Secret Love ... 53

Samuel Taylor Coleridge (1772 – 1834)
The Presence of Love ... 56
Love ... 57

Robert Southey (1774 – 1843)
Go, Valentine… ... 61

Thomas Moore (1779 – 1852)
She is far from the land… ... 62

George Gordon, Lord Byron (1788-1824)
So we'll go no more a-roving… ... 63
She walks in beauty… ... 64
When we two parted… ... 65

Alphonse de Lamartine (1790-1869)
Solitude ... 66
The Lake ... 68

Percy Bysshe Shelley (1792-1822)
To Jane ... 71
Love's Philosophy ... 72

John Clare (1793-1864)
First Love ... 73
How Can I Forget? ... 74

John Keats (1795-1821)
Bright Star ... 75
To Fanny Brawne ... 76
You say you love; but with a voice … ... 77

Franz von Schober (1796 - 1882)
By the Brook in Springtime ... 78

CONTENTS

Heinrich Heine (1797 - 1856)
The Lotus Flower	79
The Coveted Jewels	80
Unrequited Love	81
Lorelei	82

Thomas Hood 1799 - 1845)
Time of Roses	83
Ruth	84

Ludwig Rellstab (1799 - 1860)
Serenade	85

Victor Hugo (1802 – 1885)
The Journey	86

Elizabeth Barrett Browning (1806 – 1861)
If thou must love me, let it be for nought	87
How do I love thee? Let me count the ways.	88

Félix Arvers (1806 – 1850)
Sonnet	89

Alfred, Lord Tennyson (1809 - 1892)
Break, break, break…	90
Go not, happy day…	91
Birds in the high hall garden…	92
Come into the garden, Maud…	93

Edgar Allan Poe (1809 - 1849)
A Dream Within a Dream	96
Annabel Lee	97

Robert Browning (1812 – 1889)
Now	99
Life in a Love	100

George Eliot (1819 - 1880)
Sweet evenings come and go, love…	101

CONTENTS

Charles Kingsley (1819 - 1875)
A Farewell	102
Young and Old	103

Charles Baudelaire (1821 – 1867)
To a Passer-By	104
The Fountain	105
Invitation to a Journey	107
A Hemisphere In Your Hair	109
The Poison	111
One night as I lay with a wanton hussy	112
Hymn	113
A Perfect Whole	114
The Portrait	115
The Balcony	116
The Lovers' Wine	117
The Lovers' Death	118

Matthew Arnold (1822 - 1888)
Longing	119

Stephen Foster (1826 –1864)
Beautiful Dreamer	120
Jeanie with the Light Brown Hair	121

Christina Rossetti (1830 - 1894)
Remember	122
I loved you first…	123
The First Day	124
Somewhere or other there must surely be…	125
Echo	126

Emily Dickinson (1830 – 1886)
A charm invests a face…	127
That I did always love	128
For each ecstatic instant…	129
You left me, sweet, two legacies…	130
Wild nights - Wild nights!	131
If you were coming in the fall…	132

CONTENTS

Elizabeth Akers Allen (1832 - 1911)
At Last   133

William Morris (1834 - 1896)
Love is enough   134

Alfred Austin (1835 – 1913)
Love's Trinity   135

Henri Cazalis (1840 - 1909)
Florentine Serenade   136
The Antidote   137

Thomas Hardy (1840 - 1928)
Neutral Tones   138
The Voice   139

Paul Verlaine (1844 - 1896)
My Familiar Dream   140

Robert Seymour Bridges (1844 – 1930)
My delight and thy delight…   141
So sweet love seemed that April morn…   142
I will not let thee go…   143

Ella Wheeler Wilcox (1850 - 1919)
When Love Is Lost   145
Love's Coming   146
You Will Forget Me   147
Love's Language   148
I Love You   150

Oscar Wilde (1854 –1900)
To My Wife   151

Edith Nesbitt (1858 - 1924)
A Tragedy   152

A. E. Housman (1859-1936)
When the lad for longing sighs…   153
Oh, when I was in love with you…   154
When I was one-and-twenty…   155

CONTENTS

Sir Arthur Somervell (1863 –1937)
Silent Worship   156

William Butler Yeats ((1865-1939)
When you are old and grey…   157
The Cloths of Heaven   158
Down by the Salley Gardens…   159
Never Give All The Heart   160

Guillaume Apollinaire (1880 – 1918)
The Mirabeau Bridge   161

Khalil Gibran (1883 –1931)
Love One Another   162
Of Love   163
Let These Be Your Desires   164

Sara Teasdale (1884 — 1933)
The Kiss   165
I am not yours, not lost in you…   166
Alone   167
I Shall Not Care   168
After Love   169

Rupert Brooke (1887 - 1915)
Love   170
Beauty and Beauty   171

Edna St. Vincent Millay (1892 – 1950)
I think I should have loved you presently   172
When we are old…   173
Love is not all…   174
When I too long have looked upon your face…   175

Love's Epitaph (anon.)   177

Index of poets   179

Index of titles and first lines   181

Goethe bids farewell to Friederike Brion
Woodcut c. 1890 after a drawing by Eugen Klimsch (1839–1896)
(see *Welcome and Farewell,* page 47)

FOREWORD

For centuries, poets have sought to capture the elusive, multifaceted emotion we call love. From the first tentative stirrings of infatuation to the profound depths of lifelong commitment, love has been a constant muse, inspiring verses that echo through the ages.

Within these pages, you will find love in all its guises: the giddy rush of new romance, the quiet comfort of familiarity, the bittersweet ache of longing, and the devastating sting of heartbreak. Here are poems that delve into the complexities of desire, that grapple with the challenges of maintaining love in a world that often feels indifferent to its fragility.

Love, as we know, is rarely a smooth, idyllic journey. It is a tapestry woven with threads of joy and sorrow, hope and despair. These poems reflect that reality, embracing the full spectrum of human experience that love encompasses. You will encounter poems that wrestle with doubt, poems that confront loss, and poems that acknowledge the inherent imperfections within ourselves and our relationships.

But amidst the complexities, a common thread binds these diverse voices together: the unwavering belief in the power of love. Whether it's the burning passion of youth or the quiet contentment of shared memories, love has the ability to illuminate our lives, to connect us to something larger than ourselves, and to remind us of our shared humanity.

Whether you are a seasoned poetry enthusiast or a curious newcomer, this anthology will offer you a new appreciation of the power of poetry to capture the essence of love in all its many facets. Let these poems resonate with your own experiences, challenge your perspectives, and remind you of the enduring beauty and power of the human heart.

John E. Tidball, August 2025

ODE TO CASSANDRA

Come, my sweet Love, to see the rose
That but this morning did unclose
Its robe of crimson to the sun;
Can it have lost, this vesper hour,
The folds of its fair-scented flower,
Pink-blushing like my fairest one?

Alas, see here upon the ground
The crimson petals all around,
So negligently cast aside.
O Nature, whence this wanton duty
To cause a flower to shed its beauty
'Twixt dawn's first light and eventide?

My Love, heed now these words, I pray:
So long as you are blithe and gay
And your sweet youth is in full bloom,
Be sure to cherish every hour,
For careless time, as with this flower,
Will mar your beauty all too soon.

– Pierre de Ronsard (1524 – 1585)
  (translated from the French)

SONNET FOR HELEN

When you are very old, reclining in your chair
Beside the fire, unwinding wool at close of day,
Singing my verses, you in wonderment will say,
Ronsard did honour me when I was young and fair.

There is no servant who, hearing such wonders told,
Though weary from the toilsome duties of the day,
Would not wake from her sleep and rise from where she lay
To celebrate a name that Ronsard once extolled.

And when beneath the earth my mortal soul is laid
In everlasting peace beneath the myrtle's shade,
You'll sit beside the fire, a spinster bowed and bent,

Regretting that you spurned my love so long ago.
Youth is a verdant field where fragrant flowers grow:
Gather your roses now, wait not till life is spent.

– Pierre de Ronsard
   (translated from the French)

FAIR AND TRUE

Lovely kind, and kindly loving,
Such a mind were worth the moving;
Truly fair, and fairly true —
Where are all these, but in you?

Wisely kind, and kindly wise;
Blessed life, where such love lies!
Wise, and kind, and fair, and true —
Lovely live all these in you.

Sweetly dear, and dearly sweet;
Blessed, where these blessings meet!
Sweet, fair, wise, kind, blessed, true -
Blessed be all these in you!

– Nicholas Breton (c. 1542 - 1626)

ICE AND FIRE

My love is like to ice, and I to fire:
How comes it then that this her cold so great
Is not dissolved through my so hot desire,
But harder grows the more I her entreat?
Or how comes it that my exceeding heat
Is not allayed by her heart-frozen cold,
But that I burn much more in boiling sweat,
And feel my flames augmented manifold?
What more miraculous thing may be told,
That fire, which all things melts, should harden ice,
And ice, which is congeal'd with senseless cold,
Should kindle fire by wonderful device?
Such is the power of love in gentle mind,
That it can alter all the course of kind.

– Edmund Spenser (c.1552-1599)

One day I wrote her name...

One day I wrote her name upon the strand,
But came the waves and washed it away:
Again I wrote it with a second hand,
But came the tide and made my pains his prey.
"Vain man," said she, "that dost in vain essay
A mortal thing so to immortalize;
For I myself shall like to this decay,
And eke my name be wiped out likewise."
"Not so," quoth I; "let baser things devise
To lie in dust, but you shall live by fame;
My verse your virtues rare shall eternize,
And in the heavens write your glorious name:
Where, whenas Death shall all the world subdue,
Our love shall live, and later life renew."

– Edmund Spenser

My true love hath my heart....

My true love hath my heart, and I have his,
By just exchange one for the other given:
I hold his dear, and mine he cannot miss;
There never was a bargain better driven.
His heart in me keeps me and him in one;
My heart in him his thoughts and senses guides:
He loves my heart, for once it was his own;
I cherish his because in me it bides.
His heart his wound received from my sight;
My heart was wounded with his wounded heart;
For as from me on him his hurt did light,
So still, methought, in me his hurt did smart:
Both equal hurt, in this change sought our bliss,
My true love hath my heart, and I have his.

– Sir Philip Sidney (1554 - 86)

Since there's no help....

Since there's no help, come let us kiss and part;
Nay, I have done, you get no more of me,
And I am glad, yea glad with all my heart
That thus so cleanly I myself can free;
Shake hands forever, cancel all our vows,
And when we meet at any time again,
Be it not seen in either of our brows
That we one jot of former love retain.
Now at the last gasp of Love's latest breath,
When, his pulse failing, Passion speechless lies,
When Faith is kneeling by his bed of death,
And Innocence is closing up his eyes,
Now if thou wouldst, when all have given him over,
From death to life thou mightst him yet recover.

– Michael Drayton (1563-1631)

SONNET 18

Shall I compare thee to a summer's day?
Thou art more lovely and more temperate.
Rough winds do shake the darling buds of May,
And summer's lease hath all too short a date.
Sometime too hot the eye of heaven shines,
And often is his gold complexion dimmed;
And every fair from fair sometime declines,
By chance, or nature's changing course, untrimmed;
But thy eternal summer shall not fade,
Nor lose possession of that fair thou ow'st,
Nor shall death brag thou wand'rest in his shade,
When in eternal lines to Time thou grow'st.
So long as men can breathe, or eyes can see,
So long lives this, and this gives life to thee.

– William Shakespeare (1564 - 1616)

SONNET 116

Let me not to the marriage of true minds
Admit impediments. Love is not love
Which alters when it alteration finds,
Or bends with the remover to remove.
O no! it is an ever-fixèd mark
That looks on tempests and is never shaken;
It is the star to every wand'ring bark,
Whose worth's unknown, although his height be taken.
Love's not Time's fool, though rosy lips and cheeks
Within his bending sickle's compass come;
Love alters not with his brief hours and weeks,
But bears it out e'en to the edge of doom.
If this be error and upon me proved,
I never writ, nor no man ever loved.

– William Shakespeare

SONNET 130

My mistress' eyes are nothing like the sun;
Coral is far more red, than her lips' red:
If snow be white, why then her breasts are dun;
If hairs be wires, black wires grow on her head.
I have seen roses damasked, red and white,
But no such roses see I in her cheeks;
And in some perfumes is there more delight
Than in the breath that from my mistress reeks.
I love to hear her speak, yet well I know
That music hath a far more pleasing sound:
I grant I never saw a goddess go,
My mistress, when she walks, treads on the ground:
And yet by heaven, I think my love as rare,
As any she belied with false compare.

– William Shakespeare

SONNET 147

My love is as a fever, longing still
For that which longer nurseth the disease,
Feeding on that which doth preserve the ill,
Th' uncertain sickly appetite to please.
My reason, the physician to my love,
Angry that his prescriptions are not kept,
Hath left me, and I desperate now approve
Desire is death, which physic did except.
Past cure I am, now reason is past care,
And frantic-mad with evermore unrest;
My thoughts and my discourse as madmen's are,
At random from the truth vainly expressed:
For I have sworn thee fair, and thought thee bright,
Who art as black as hell, as dark as night.

– William Shakespeare

THE PASSIONATE SHEPHERD TO HIS LOVE

Come live with me, and be my love,
And we will all the pleasures prove,
That hills and valleys, dales and fields,
And all the craggy mountain yields.

There we will sit upon the rocks,
And see the shepherds feed their flocks
By shallow rivers, to whose falls
Melodious birds sing madrigals.

And I will make thee beds of roses,
With a thousand fragrant posies,
A cap of flowers and a kirtle
Embroidered all with leaves of myrtle;

A gown made of the finest wool,
Which from our pretty lambs we pull;
Fair lined slippers for the cold,
With buckles of the purest gold;

A belt of straw and ivy buds,
With coral clasps and amber studs;
And if these pleasures may thee move,
Come live with me, and be my love.

Thy silver dishes for thy meat
As precious as the gods do eat,
Shall on an ivory table be
Prepared each day for thee and me.

The shepherd swains shall dance and sing
For thy delight each May-morning:
If these delights thy mind may move,
Then live with me, and be my love.

– Christopher Marlowe (1564 – 1593)

WHO EVER LOVED, THAT LOVED NOT AT FIRST SIGHT?

It lies not in our power to love or hate,
For will in us is overruled by fate.
When two are stripped, long ere the course begin,
We wish that one should love, the other win;
And one especially do we affect
Of two gold ingots, like in each respect:
The reason no man knows, let it suffice,
What we behold is censured by our eyes.
Where both deliberate, the love is slight:
Who ever loved, that loved not at first sight?

– Christopher Marlowe

AMARYLLIS

I care not for these ladies that must be wooed and prayed;
Give me kind Amaryllis, the wanton country maid.
Nature Art disdaineth; her beauty is her own,
Who when we court and kiss, she cries: forsooth, let go!
But when we come where comfort is, she never will say no.

If I love Amaryllis, she gives me fruit and flowers;
But if we love these ladies, we must give golden showers.
Give them gold that sell love, give me the nut-brown lass,
Who when we court and kiss, she cries: forsooth, let go!
But when we come where comfort is, she never will say no.

These ladies must have pillows and beds by strangers wrought.
Give me a bower of willows, of moss and leaves unbought,
And fresh Amaryllis with milk and honey fed,
Who when we court and kiss, she cries: forsooth, let go!
But when we come where comfort is, she never will say no.

– Thomas Campion (c. 1567–1619)

SONG TO CELIA – I

Come, my Celia, let us prove
While we may the sports of love;
Time will not be ours forever,
He at length our good will sever.
Spend not then his gifts in vain;
Suns that set may rise again,
But if once we lose this light,
'Tis with us perpetual night.
Why should we defer our joys?
Fame and rumour are but toys
Cannot we delude the eyes
Of a few poor household spies?
Or his easier ears beguile,
So removed by our wile?
'Tis no sin love's fruits to steal;
But the sweet theft to reveal,
To be taken, to be seen,
These have crimes accounted been.

– Ben Jonson (1572 - 1637)

SONG TO CELIA – II

Drink to me only with thine eyes,
And I will pledge with mine;
Or leave a kiss within the cup,
And I'll not ask for wine.
The thirst that from the soul doth rise
Doth ask a drink divine;
But might I of Jove's nectar sip,
I would not change for thine.

I sent thee late a rosy wreath,
Not so much honouring thee,
As giving it a hope that there
It would not withered be.
But thou thereon didst only breathe
And send'st it back to me:
Since when it grows, and smells, I swear,
Not of itself, but thee.

– Ben Jonson

Love not me for comely grace...

Love not me for comely grace,
For my pleasing eye or face,
Nor for any outward part:
No, nor for a constant heart!
For these may fail or turn to ill:
Should thou and I sever.

Keep, therefore, a true woman's eye,
And love me still, but know not why!
So hast thou the same reason still
To dote upon me ever.

– John Wilbye (1574 – 1638)

Take, oh, take those lips away…

Take, oh, take those lips away
That so sweetly were forsworn
And those eyes, like break of day,
Lights that do mislead the morn;
But my kisses bring again,
Seals of love, though sealed in vain.

Hide, oh, hide those hills of snow,
Which thy frozen bosom bears,
On whose tops the pinks that grow
Are of those that April wears;
But first set my poor heart free,
Bound in those icy chains by thee.

– John Fletcher (1579–1625)

There is a lady sweet and kind…

There is a lady sweet and kind,
Was never face so pleas'd my mind;
I did but see her passing by,
And yet I love her till I die.

Her gesture, motion, and her smiles,
Her wit, her voice, my heart beguiles,
Beguiles my heart, I know not why,
And yet I love her till I die.

Her free behaviour, winning looks,
Will make a lawyer burn his books;
I touch'd her not, alas! not I,
And yet I love her till I die.

Had I her fast betwixt mine arms,
Judge you that think such sports were harms,
Were't any harm? no, no, fie, fie,
For I will love her till I die.

Should I remain confinèd there
So long as Phoebus in his sphere,
I to request, she to deny,
Yet would I love her till I die.

Cupid is wingèd and doth range
Her country, so my love doth change:
But change she earth, or change she sky,
Yet will I love her till I die.

– Thomas Ford (1580–1648)

TO VIRGINS, TO MAKE MUCH OF TIME

Gather ye rose-buds while ye may,
Old Time is still a flying:
And this same flower that smiles today,
Tomorrow will be dying.

The glorious lamp of heaven, the sun,
The higher he's a getting;
The sooner will his race be run,
And nearer he's to setting.

That age is best, which is the first,
When youth and blood are warmer;
But being spent, the worse, and worst
Times, still succeed the former.

Then be not coy, but use your time;
And while ye may, go marry:
For having lost but once your prime,
You may forever tarry.

– Robert Herrick (1591-1674)

SWEET DISORDER

A sweet disorder in the dress
Kindles in clothes a wantonness:
A lawn about the shoulders thrown
Into a fine distraction --
An erring lace, which here and there
Enthrals the crimson stomacher --
A cuff neglectful, and thereby
Ribbands to flow confusedly --
A winning wave, deserving note,
In the tempestuous petticoat --
A careless shoe-string, in whose tie
I see a wild civility --
Do more bewitch me than when art
Is too precise in every part.

– Robert Herrick

Love bade me welcome...

Love bade me welcome, yet my soul drew back,
Guilty of dust and sin.
But quick-eyed Love, observing me grow slack
From my first entrance in,
Drew nearer to me, sweetly questioning,
If I lacked any thing.

A guest, I answered, worthy to be here:
Love said, You shall be he.
I the unkind, ungrateful? Ah my dear,
I cannot look on thee.
Love took my hand, and smiling did reply,
Who made the eyes but I?

Truth Lord, but I have marred them: let my shame
Go where it doth deserve.
And know you not, says Love, who bore the blame?
My dear, then I will serve.
You must sit down, says Love, and taste my meat:
So I did sit and eat.

– George Herbert (1593 – 1633)

I prithee send me back my heart...

I prithee send me back my heart,
Since I cannot have thine;
For if from yours you will not part,
Why, then, shouldst thou have mine?

Yet now I think on't, let it lie,
To find it were in vain;
For thou hast a thief in either eye
Would steal it back again.

Why should two hearts in one breast lie,
And yet not lodge together?
O Love! where is thy sympathy,
If thus our breasts thou sever?

But love is such a mystery,
I cannot find it out;
For when I think I'm best resolved,
I then am in most doubt.

Then farewell care, and farewell woe;
I will no longer pine;
For I'll believe I have her heart,
As much as she hath mine.

– Sir John Suckling (1609 – 1641)

TO MY DEAR AND LOVING HUSBAND

If ever two were one, then surely we.
If ever man were lov'd by wife, then thee;
If ever wife was happy in a man,
Compare with me ye women if you can.
I prize thy love more than whole Mines of gold,
Or all the riches that the East doth hold.
My love is such that Rivers cannot quench,
Nor ought but love from thee, give recompense.
Thy love is such I can no way repay,
The heavens reward thee manifold I pray.
Then while we live, in love let's so persever,
That when we live no more, we may live ever.

– Anne Bradstreet (1612 – 1672)

Tell me not, Sweet, I am unkind…

Tell me not, Sweet, I am unkind
For, from the nunnery
Of thy chaste breast, and quiet mind,
To war and arms I fly.

True, a new mistress now I chase,
The first foe in the field;
And with a stronger faith- embrace
A sword, a horse, a shield.

Yet this unconstancy is such
As you too shall adore;
For, I could not love thee, Dear, so much,
Loved I not honour more.

– Richard Lovelace (1617 – 1657)

HIDDEN FLAME

Feed a flame within, which so torments me
That it both pains my heart, and yet contains me:
'Tis such a pleasing smart, and I so love it,
That I had rather die than once remove it.

Yet he, for whom I grieve, shall never know it;
My tongue does not betray, nor my eyes show it.
Not a sigh, nor a tear, my pain discloses,
But they fall silently, like dew on roses.

Thus, to prevent my Love from being cruel,
My heart's the sacrifice, as 'tis the fuel;
And while I suffer this to give him quiet,
My faith rewards my love, though he deny it.

On his eyes will I gaze, and there delight me;
While I conceal my love no frown can fright me.
To be more happy I dare not aspire,
Nor can I fall more low, mounting no higher.

– John Dryden (1631 - 1700)

LOVE AND LIFE

All my past life is mine no more,
The flying hours are gone,
Like transitory dreams given o'er,
Whose images are kept in store
By memory alone.

Whatever is to come is not;
How can it then be mine?
The present moment's all my lot;
And that, as fast as it is got,
Phyllis, is wholly thine.

Then talk not of inconstancy,
False hearts, and broken vows;
If I, by miracle, can be
This live-long minute true to thee,
'Tis all that heaven allows.

– John Wilmot (1647 – 1680)

EVENING ODE

Evening now from purple wings
Sheds the grateful gifts she brings;
Brilliant drops bedeck the mead,
Cooling breezes shake the reed;
Shake the reed, and curl the stream
Silver'd o'er with Cynthia's beam;
Near the chequer'd, lonely grove,
Hears, and keeps thy secrets, love!
Stella, thither let us stray,
Lightly o'er the dewy way.
Phoebus drives his burning car,
Hence, my lovely Stella, far;
In his stead, the queen of night
Round us pours a lambent light:
Light that seems but just to show
Breasts that beat, and cheeks that glow;
Let us now, in whisper'd joy,
Evening's silent hours employ,
Silent best, and conscious shades,
Please the hearts that love invades,
Other pleasures give them pain,
Lovers all but love disdain.

– Samuel Johnson (1709 – 1784)

THE WINTER'S WALK

Behold, my fair, where'er we rove,
What dreary prospects round us rise,
The naked hill, the leafless grove,
The hoary ground, the frowning skies.

Nor only through the wasted plain,
Stern Winter is thy force confess'd;
Still wider spreads thy horrid reign,
I feel thy power usurp my breast.

Enlivening hope, and fond desire,
Resign the heart to spleen and care;
Scarce frighted love maintains her fire,
And rapture saddens to despair.

In groundless hope, and causeless fear,
Unhappy man! behold thy doom;
Still changing with the changeful year
The slave of sunshine and of gloom.

Tired with vain joys, the false alarms,
With mental and corporeal strife,
Snatch me, my Stella, to thy arms,
And screen me from the ills of life.

– Samuel Johnson

SUMMER

O Phoebus! down the western sky,
Far hence diffuse thy burning ray,
Thy light to distant worlds supply,
And wake them to the cares of day.

Come, gentle Eve, the friend of care,
Come, Cynthia, lovely queen of night!
Refresh me with a cooling breeze,
And cheer me with a lambent light.

Lay me, where o'er the verdant ground
Her living carpet Nature spreads;
Where the green bower with roses crown'd,
In showers its fragrant foliage spreads.

Improve the peaceful hour with wine,
Let music die along the grove;
Around the bowl let myrtles twine,
And every strain be tuned to love.

Come, Stella, queen of all my heart!
Come, born to fill its vast desires!
Thy looks perpetual joy impart,
Thy voice perpetual love inspires.

Whilst all my wish and thine complete,
By turns we languish and we burn,
Let sighing gales our sights repeat,
Our murmurs - murmuring brooks return.

Let me when Nature calls to rest,
And blushing skies the morn foretell,
Sink on the down of Stella's breast,
And bid the waking world farewell.

– Samuel Johnson

TO STELLA

Not the soft sighs of vernal gales,
The fragrance of the flow'ry vales,
The murmurs of the crystal rill,
The vocal grove, the verdant hill;
Not all their charms, though all unite,
Can touch my bosom with delight.

Not all the gems on India's shore,
Not all Peru's unbounded store,
Not all the power, nor all the fame,
That heroes, kings, or poets claim;
Nor knowledge, which the learn'd approve;
To form one wish my soul can move.

Yet nature's charms allure my eyes,
And knowledge, wealth, and fame I prize;
Fame, wealth, and knowledge I obtain,
Nor seek I nature's charms in vain;
In lovely Stella all combine;
And, lovely Stella! thou art mine.

– Samuel Johnson

WOULD YOU WERE HERE!

I think of you when rays of gold
Caress the sea.
I think of you when silver moonbeams
Kiss the lea.

I see you on the lonely road
At break of day;
At dusk, when on my homeward path
I wend my way.

I hear your voice in woodland
When a gentle breeze
Springs up to send a whisper
Through the silent trees.

You're by my side; though you are far,
Yet you are near!
The sun goes down; stars light my path:
Would you were here!

– Johann Wolfgang von Goethe (1749 - 1832)
 (translated from the German)

WELCOME AND FAREWELL

My heart beat fast: to horse! away!
No sooner thought than it was done;
The evening held earth in its sway,
And night upon the mountains hung.
Shrouded in mist there stood the oak,
A giant of colossal size,
While darkness pierced the undergrowth
With myriad atramentous eyes.

Behind a clouded hill the moon
Endeavoured timidly to peer;
On wings of whispered song the wind
Played eerily about my ear;
Night spawned a thousand monsters there,
Yet blithe in spirit on I pressed;
Within my veins what burning fire!
What glowing ardour in my breast!

I saw you, and such tender joy
Flowed from your sweet gaze to my own;
My heart was wholly at your side,
Each breath I took for you alone.
A gentle shade of vernal rose
Upon your features I observed;
Such tenderness for me — ye gods!
So hoped for yet so undeserved!

But with the morning sun's first light
Adieu's sweet sorrow gripped my heart:
In those last kisses what delight!
In those dear eyes what bitter smart!
I left. Your parting gaze was blurred
By tears your heart could not suppress,
And yet what joy it is to love!
And to be loved, ye gods, what bliss!

– Johann Wolfgang von Goethe
  (translated from the German)

THE LASS OF RICHMOND HILL

On Richmond Hill there lives a lass
More bright than May Day morn
Whose charms all other maids surpass,
A rose without a thorn.
This lass so neat, with smile so sweet
Has won my right good will,
I'd crowns resign to call thee mine,
Sweet lass of Richmond Hill.

Ye zephyrs gay that fan the air
And wanton thro' the grove,
Oh whisper to my charming fair
I'd die for her I love.
This lass so neat, with smile so sweet
Has won my right good will,
I'd crowns resign to call thee mine,
Sweet lass of Richmond Hill.

How happy will the shepherd be
Who calls this nymph his own?
Oh, may her choice be fixed on me,
Mine's fix'd on her alone
This lass so neat, with smile so sweet
Has won my right good will,
I'd crowns resign to call thee mine,
Sweet lass of Richmond Hill.

– Leonard McNally (1752 –1820)

THE GARDEN OF LOVE

I went to the Garden of Love.
And saw what I never had seen:
A Chapel was built in the midst,
Where I used to play on the green.

And the gates of this Chapel were shut,
And "Thou Shalt Not", writ over the door;
So I turn'd to the Garden of Love,
That so many sweet flowers bore,

And I saw it filled with graves,
And tombstones where flowers should be:
And Priests in black gowns, were walking their rounds,
And binding with briars, my joys & desires.

– William Blake (1757 – 1827)

MY PRETTY ROSE TREE

A flower was offered to me:
Such a flower as May never bore.
But I said "I've a Pretty Rose-tree",
And I passed the sweet flower o'er.

Then I went to my Pretty Rose-tree:
To tend her by day and by night.
But my Rose turn'd away with jealousy:
And her thorns were my only delight.

– William Blake

A RED, RED ROSE

O my Luve's like a red, red rose
That's newly sprung in June:
O my Luve's like the melodie
That's sweetly play'd in tune.

As fair art thou, my bonnie lass,
So deep in luve am I:
And I will luve thee still, my dear,
Till a' the seas gang dry:

Till a' the seas gang dry, my dear,
And the rocks melt wi' the sun;
I will luve thee still, my dear,
While the sands o' life shall run.

And fare thee weel, my only Luve!
And fare thee weel a while!
And I will come again, my Luve,
Tho' it were ten thousand mile.

– Robert Burns (1759-1796)

THE PARTING KISS

Humid seal of soft affections,
Tenderest pledge of future bliss,
Dearest tie of young connections,
Love's first snowdrop, virgin kiss!

Speaking silence, dumb confession,
Passion's birth, and infant's play,
Dove-like fondness, chaste concession,
Glowing dawn of future day!

Sorrowing joy, Adieu's last action,
(Lingering lips must now disjoin),
What words can ever speak affection
So thrilling and sincere as thine!

– Robert Burns

SECRET LOVE

Not one kind look....one friendly word!
Wilt thou in chilling silence sit;
Nor through the social hour afford
One cheering smile, or beam of wit?

Yet still, absorbed in studious care,
Neglect to waste one look on me;
For then my happy eyes may dare
To gaze and dwell unchecked on thee.

And still in silence sit, nor deign
One gentle precious word to say;
For silent I may then remain,
Nor let my voice my soul betray.

This faltering voice, these conscious eyes,
My throbbing heart too plainly speak:
There timid hopeless passion lies,
And bids it silence keep, and break .

To me how dear this twilight hour,
Cheered by the faggot's varying blaze!
If this be mine, I ask no more
On morn's refulgent light to gaze:

For now, while on HIS glowing cheek
I see the fire's red radiance fall,
The darkest seat I softly seek,
And gaze on HIM , unseen by all.

His folded arms, his studious brow,
His thoughtful eye, unmarked, I see;
Nor could his voice or words bestow
So dear, so true a joy on me.

SECRET LOVE

But he forgets that I am near....
Fame, future fame, in thought he seeks:
To him ambition's paths appear,
And bright the sun of science breaks.

His heart with ardent hope is filled;
His prospects full of beauty bloom:
But, oh! my heart despair has chilled,
My only prospect is....the tomb!

One only boon from Heaven I claim,
And may it grant the fond desire!
That I may live to hear his fame,
And in that throb of joy expire.

Oft hast thou marked my chilling eye,
And mourned my cold reserve to see,
Resolved the fickle friend to fly,
Who seemed unjust to worth and thee:

While I, o'erjoyed, thy anger saw....
Blest proof I had not tried in vain
To give imperious passion law,
And hide my bosom's conscious pain.

But when night's sheltering darkness came,
And none the conscious wretch could view,
How fiercely burned the smothered flame!
How deep was every sigh I drew!

Yet still to thee I'll clothe my brow
In all that jealous pride requires;
My look the type of Ætna's snow....
My heart, of Ætna's secret fires.

SECRET LOVE

His frame with strong emotion shook,
And kindness tuned each faltering word;
While I, surprised, with anxious look
The meaning of his glance explored.

One little moment, short as blest,
Compassion Love's soft semblance wore;
My meagre form he fondly pressed,
And on his beating bosom bore.

But soon my too experienced heart
Read nought but generous pity there;
I felt presumptuous hope depart,
And all again was dark despair.

Yet still, in memory still, my heart
Lives o'er that fleeting bliss again;
I feel his glance, his touch, impart
Emotion through each bursting vein.

And "Once ," I cry, "those eyes so sweet
On me with fondness deigned to shine;
For once I felt his bosom beat
Against the conscious throbs of mine!"

Nor shall the dear remembrance die
While aught of life to me is given;
But soothe my last convulsive sigh,
And be, till then, my joy....my heaven!

– Amelia Opie (1769 – 1853)

THE PRESENCE OF LOVE

And in Life's noisiest hour,
There whispers still the ceaseless Love of Thee,
The heart's Self-solace and soliloquy.

You mould my Hopes, you fashion me within;
And to the leading Love-throb in the Heart
Thro' all my Being, thro' my pulse's beat;
You lie in all my many Thoughts, like Light,
Like the fair light of Dawn, or summer Eve
On rippling Stream, or cloud-reflecting Lake.

And looking to the Heaven, that bends above you,
How oft! I bless the Lot that made me love you.

– Samuel Taylor Coleridge (1772 – 1834)

LOVE

All thoughts, all passions, all delights,
Whatever stirs this mortal frame,
All are but ministers of Love,
And feed his sacred flame.

Oft in my waking dreams do I
Live o'er again that happy hour,
When midway on the mount I lay,
Beside the ruined tower.

The moonshine, stealing o'er the scene
Had blended with the lights of eve;
And she was there, my hope, my joy,
My own dear Genevieve!

She leant against the armèd man,
The statue of the armèd knight;
She stood and listened to my lay,
Amid the lingering light.

Few sorrows hath she of her own,
My hope! my joy! my Genevieve!
She loves me best, whene'er I sing
The songs that make her grieve.

I played a soft and doleful air,
I sang an old and moving story—
An old rude song, that suited well
That ruin wild and hoary.

She listened with a flitting blush,
With downcast eyes and modest grace;
For well she knew, I could not choose
But gaze upon her face.

LOVE

I told her of the Knight that wore
Upon his shield a burning brand;
And that for ten long years he wooed
The Lady of the Land.

I told her how he pined: and ah!
The deep, the low, the pleading tone
With which I sang another's love,
Interpreted my own.

She listened with a flitting blush,
With downcast eyes, and modest grace;
And she forgave me, that I gazed
Too fondly on her face!

But when I told the cruel scorn
That crazed that bold and lovely Knight,
And that he crossed the mountain-woods,
Nor rested day nor night;

That sometimes from the savage den,
And sometimes from the darksome shade,
And sometimes starting up at once
In green and sunny glade, —

There came and looked him in the face
An angel beautiful and bright;
And that he knew it was a Fiend,
This miserable Knight!

And that unknowing what he did,
He leaped amid a murderous band,
And saved from outrage worse than death
The Lady of the Land!

LOVE

And how she wept, and clasped his knees;
And how she tended him in vain —
And ever strove to expiate
The scorn that crazed his brain; —

And that she nursed him in a cave;
And how his madness went away,
When on the yellow forest-leaves
A dying man he lay; —

His dying words — but when I reached
That tenderest strain of all the ditty,
My faultering voice and pausing harp
Disturbed her soul with pity!

All impulses of soul and sense
Had thrilled my guileless Genevieve;
The music and the doleful tale,
The rich and balmy eve;

And hopes, and fears that kindle hope,
An undistinguishable throng,
And gentle wishes long subdued,
Subdued and cherished long!

She wept with pity and delight,
She blushed with love, and virgin-shame;
And like the murmur of a dream,
I heard her breathe my name.

Her bosom heaved — she stepped aside,
As conscious of my look she stepped —
Then suddenly, with timorous eye
She fled to me and wept.

LOVE

She half enclosed me with her arms,
She pressed me with a meek embrace;
And bending back her head, looked up,
And gazed upon my face.

'Twas partly love, and partly fear,
And partly 'twas a bashful art,
That I might rather feel, than see,
The swelling of her heart.

I calmed her fears, and she was calm,
And told her love with virgin pride;
And so I won my Genevieve,
My bright and beauteous Bride.

– Samuel Taylor Coleridge

GO, VALENTINE

Go, Valentine, and tell that lovely maid
Whom fancy still will portray to my sight,
How here I linger in this sullen shade,
This dreary gloom of dull monastic night;
Say, that every joy of life remote
At evening's closing hour I quit the throng,
Listening in solitude the ring-dome's note,
Who pours like me her solitary song;
Say, that of her absence calls the sorrowing sigh;
Say, that of all her charms I love to speak,
In fancy feel the magic of her eye,
In fancy view the smile illume her cheek,
Court the lone hour when silence stills the grove,
And heave the sigh of memory and of love.

– Robert Southey (1774 – 1843)

She is far from the land...

She is far from the land, where her young hero sleeps,
And lovers are round her, sighing;
But coldly she turns from their gaze, and weeps,
For her heart in his grave is lying!
She sings the wild song of her dear native plains,
Every note which he lov'd awaking
Ah! little they think, who delight in her strains,
How the heart of the Minstrel is breaking!

He had lov'd for his love, for his country he died,
They were all that to life had entwin'd him,
Nor soon shall the tears of his country be dried,
Nor long will his love stay behind him.

Oh! make her a grave, where the sun-beams rest,
When they promise a glorious morrow;
They'll shine o'er her sleep, like a smile from the West,
From her own lov'd Island of sorrow!

– Thomas Moore (1779 – 1852)

So we'll go no more a-roving…

So, we'll go no more a-roving
So late into the night,
Though the heart be still as loving
And the moon be still as bright.

For the sword outwears its sheath
And the soul wears out the breast
And a heart must pause to breathe
And love itself have rest.

Though the night was made for loving
And the day returns too soon,
Yet, we'll go no more a-roving
By the light of the moon.

– George Gordon, Lord Byron (1788-1824)

She walks in beauty...

She walks in beauty, like the night
Of cloudless climes and starry skies;
And all that's best of dark and bright
Meet in her aspect and her eyes:
Thus mellowed to that tender light
Which heaven to gaudy day denies.

One shade the more, one ray the less,
Had half impaired the nameless grace
Which waves in every raven tress,
Or softly lightens o'er her face;
Where thoughts serenely sweet express
How pure, how dear their dwelling place.

And on that cheek, and o'er that brow,
So soft, so calm, yet eloquent,
The smiles that win, the tints that glow,
But tell of days in goodness spent,
A mind at peace with all below,
A heart whose love is innocent!

– George Gordon, Lord Byron

When we two parted...

When we two parted
In silence and tears,
Half broken-hearted,
To sever for years,
Pale grew thy cheek and cold,
Colder thy kiss;
Truly that hour foretold
Sorrow to this.

The dew of the morning
Sank chill on my brow
It felt like the warning
Of what I feel now.
Thy vows are all broken,
And light is thy fame:
I hear thy name spoken,
And share in its shame.

They name thee before me,
A knell to mine ear;
A shudder comes o'er me
Why wert thou so dear?
They know not I knew thee,
Who knew thee too well:
Long, long shall I rue thee
Too deeply to tell.

In secret we met
In silence I grieve
That thy heart could forget,
Thy spirit deceive.
If I should meet thee
After long years,
How should I greet thee?
With silence and tears.

– George Gordon, Lord Byron

SOLITUDE

Often, on the hillside, in the old oak's shade,
I sit, wistfully pensive, in summer's evening glow;
Across the open plain o'er which my eyes have strayed,
An ever-changing vista stretches out below.

Here, the tumultuous river's foaming billows break;
Meandering, it sinks into the gloom afar;
There, motionless, the dormant waters of the lake
Reflect in the azure the rising evening star.

Upon the mountain's crest, crowned by a sombre wood,
A final glimmer in the twilight grows more dim,
And the ethereal chariot of the queen of shade
Ascends, and renders pale the skyline's tranquil rim.

Meanwhile, issuing forth from a mediaeval spire,
The sound of sacred music permeates the air,
The wayfarer takes pause, and the old rustic bell
Blends with the day's last sounds its saintly, solemn air.

But my soul is not moved by these harmonious scenes
That on my listless soul no charm or joy can shed;
Like a wandering shadow I contemplate the earth:
The sun of living souls no longer warms the dead.

From hill to hill in vain I turn my restless gaze;
From south to north, from daybreak to the setting sun,
My eyes scan every part of the immense expanse,
And I think: "Nowhere here can sorrow be undone."

What good to me are valleys, mansions, cottages,
Vain objects for whose beauty I no longer care?
Beloved solitude of forests, rivers, rocks,
One mortal soul is absent, and all is barren there.

SOLITUDE

Whether the sun begins or ends its daily course,
I follow its migration with an indifferent gaze;
Whether it sets or rises in bright or sombre skies,
What care I for the sun? I weary of my days.

If I could follow it in its relentless run,
My eyes would only see deserted, barren land;
I wish for nothing that's illumined by the sun,
On all of vast creation I make no demand.

And yet perhaps beyond the limits of its sphere,
In places where the true sun lights up other skies,
If only I could leave my body to the earth,
What I have dreamed of would appear before my eyes!

There, I would grow drunk at the spring for which I yearn;
There, I would find once more both hope and love again,
And that ideal estate which every soul desires,
That has no name while we sojourn in earth's domain.

If I could only, on Aurora's chariot,
Vague object of my fancy, be transported to thee!
Why do I still remain in exile on the earth?
There is no harmony between the earth and me.

The withered autumn leaf that lies upon the heath
Is snatched from whence it fell and borne away upon
A gust of evening wind; I am a withered leaf:
O take me with you too, unbridled Aquilon!

– Alphonse De Lamartine (1790-1869)
  (translated from the French)

THE LAKE

Thus carried ever forth to undiscovered shores,
Into eternal night forever borne away,
Can we not once upon the vast ocean of time
Drop anchor for a day?

Oh lake, the present year has scarcely run its course,
By cherished waves that she ought once more to have seen,
Look! I have come alone to sit on this rock where
She used to sit and dream!

Thus did your waters roar beneath these lofty cliffs,
Against their rugged flanks your surging billows beat,
While gusts of wind dispersed the lather of their spray
On her beloved feet.

One night, do you recall? we drifted silently;
Afloat beneath the lake's celestial canopy,
With just the sound of oars that skimmed the tranquil deep
In rhythmic harmony.

All of a sudden, accents unknown to the earth
From your enchanted shores echoed imploringly;
Your waters lent their ear, and that beloved voice
Let fall this fervent plea:

"O Time! Suspend your flight, and you, propitious hours,
Suspend your daily race!
Let us have pause to taste the transient delights
Of our most happy days!

"So many wretched souls here on this earth implore;
Receive them in your flow;
Take with their days the pain and anguish they endure;
Let the happy go.

THE LAKE

"But I request in vain those moments to retain;
Time shuns me in its flight;
I say unto the night: Slow down! and yet the dawn
Will dissipate the night.

"Therefore let's love, let's love! Let's hasten to enjoy
The hour that soon is gone!
Man has no port of call, for time there is no shore!
It flows, and we pass on!"

Harsh time, how can it be that moments of sweet bliss,
When love pours from its urn great floods of happiness,
Can take their leave from us so much more rapidly
Than days of wretchedness?

What! Can we then not fix at least a trace of it?
What! Gone forever! What! Does nothing now remain?
Those moments granted us, those moments now erased,
Will not return again!

Eternity, past time, dark chasms, nothingness,
What do you with the days that you have swallowed up?
Speak! Will you give us back those ecstasies sublime
That you have snatched from us?

O Lake, your silent rocks, your grottos, your dark woods,
You, whom time spares or even can rejuvenate,
Fair Nature, will you keep at least the memory
Of this enchanted night!

Be it in your repose or in your raging storms,
Fair Lake, and in the joy of laughing hillsides, and
In these dark pine trees, and in these primeval rocks
That o'er your waters stand;

THE LAKE

Be it in zephyr breezes that tremble as they pass,
In sounds that from your banks ring out from shore to shore,
Or in the silver glow of stars that on your waters
Their gentle radiance pour.

May the lamenting wind, the sighing of the reeds,
The balmy breeze that wafts its fragrance from above,
May everything we see, and hear, and live, and breathe,
All say: here they did love!

– Alphonse De Lamartine
   (translated from the French)

TO JANE

The keen stars were twinkling,
And the fair moon was rising among them,
Dear Jane.
The guitar was tinkling,
But the notes were not sweet till you sung them
Again.

As the moon's soft splendour
O'er the faint cold starlight of Heaven
Is thrown,
So your voice most tender
To the strings without soul had then given
Its own.

The stars will awaken,
Though the moon sleep a full hour later
To-night;
No leaf will be shaken
Whilst the dews of your melody scatter
Delight.

Though the sound overpowers,
Sing again, with your dear voice revealing
A tone
Of some world far from ours,
Where music and moonlight and feeling
Are one.

– Percy Bysshe Shelley (1792 – 1822)

LOVE'S PHILOSOPHY

The fountains mingle with the river
And the rivers with the ocean,
The winds of heaven mix for ever
With a sweet emotion;
Nothing in the world is single;
All things by a law divine
In one spirit meet and mingle.
Why not I with thine? —

See the mountains kiss high heaven
And the waves clasp one another;
No sister-flower would be forgiven
If it disdained its brother;
And the sunlight clasps the earth
And the moonbeams kiss the sea:
What is all this sweet work worth
If thou kiss not me?

– Percy Bysshe Shelley

FIRST LOVE

I ne'er was struck before that hour
With love so sudden and so sweet,
Her face it bloomed like a sweet flower
And stole my heart away complete.
My face turned pale as deadly pale,
My legs refused to walk away,
And when she looked, what could I ail?
My life and all seemed turned to clay.

And then my blood rushed to my face
And took my eyesight quite away,
The trees and bushes round the place
Seemed midnight at noonday.
I could not see a single thing,
Words from my eyes did start —
They spoke as chords do from the string,
And blood burnt round my heart.

Are flowers the winter's choice?
Is love's bed always snow?
She seemed to hear my silent voice,
Not love's appeals to know.
I never saw so sweet a face
As that I stood before.
My heart has left its dwelling-place
And can return no more.

– John Clare (1793-1864)

HOW CAN I FORGET?

That farewell voice of love is never heard again
Yet I remember it and think on it with pain
I see the place she spoke when passing by
The flowers were blooming as her form drew nigh
That voice is gone with every pleasing tone
Loved but one moment and the next alone
Farewell the winds repeated as she went
Walking in silence through the grassy bent
The wild flowers they ne'er look'd so sweet before
Bowed in far[e] wells to her they'll see no more
In this same spot the wild flowers bloom the same
In scent and hue and shape aye even name
Twas here she said farewell and no one yet
Has so sweet spoken — How can I forget?

– John Clare

BRIGHT STAR

Bright star, would I were stedfast as thou art--
Not in lone splendour hung aloft the night
And watching, with eternal lids apart,
Like nature's patient, sleepless Eremite,
The moving waters at their priestlike task
Of pure ablution round earth's human shores,
Or gazing on the new soft-fallen mask
Of snow upon the mountains and the moors
No--yet still stedfast, still unchangeable,
Pillow'd upon my fair love's ripening breast,
To feel for ever its soft fall and swell,
Awake for ever in a sweet unrest,
Still, still to hear her tender-taken breath,
And so live ever — or else swoon to death.

– John Keats (1795 – 1821)

TO FANNY BRAWNE

I cry your mercy – pity – love! – aye, love!
Merciful love that tantalizes not,
One-thoughted, never-wandering, guileless love,
Unmasked, and being seen -without a blot!
O! let me have thee whole, -all -all -be mine!
That shape, that fairness, that sweet minor zest
Of love, your kiss, -those hands, those eyes divine,
That warm, white, lucent, million-pleasured breast,
Yourself - your soul - in pity give me all,
Withhold no atom's atom or I die,
Or living on, perhaps, your wretched thrall,
Forget, in the mist of idle misery,
Life's purposes, -the palate of my mind
Losing its gust, and my ambition blind!

– John Keats

You say you love; but with a voice ...

You say you love; but with a voice
Chaster than a nun's, who singeth
The soft vespers to herself
While the chime-bell ringeth —
O love me truly!

You say you love; but with a smile
Cold as sunrise in September,
As you were Saint Cupid's nun,
And kept his weeks of Ember —
O love me truly!

You say you love; but then your lips
Coral tinted teach no blisses,
More than coral in the sea —
They never pout for kisses —
O love me truly!

You say you love; but then your hand
No soft squeeze for squeeze returneth;
It is like a statue's, dead, —
While mine for passion burneth —
O love me truly!

O breathe a word or two of fire!
Smile, as if those words should burn me,
Squeeze as lovers should — O kiss
And in thy heart inurn me —
O love me truly!

– John Keats

BY THE BROOK IN SPRINGTIME

The brook has shed its icy crust
And blithely flows the vernal stream;
The zephyr breezes waft anew
And moss and grass are fresh and green.

Alone, in sombre mood, I walk
Beside the babbling brook again;
Yet all the beauties of the earth
Do nothing to assuage my pain.

Cold winds now blow within my soul;
All hope has faded from my mind;
E'en though I find a little flower,
Blue, like the ones my memories find.

- Franz Von Schober (1796 - 1882)
  (translated from the German)

THE LOTUS FLOWER

The lotus flower is anxious
Beneath the bright sun's light;
Her head inclined in slumber,
She waits to greet the night.

The moon is her companion,
He wakes her with his rays,
And she unveils her flower-face
Devoutly to his gaze.

She blooms, and glows, and fervently
Looks to the sky above,
Fragrantly, tearfully trembling
With the joy and the sorrow of love.

– Heinrich Heine (1797 - 1856)
    (translated from the German)

THE COVETED JEWELS

Your eyes are like two sapphires,
So blue, so pure, so sweet!
And three times lucky is the man
Whom they with ardour greet!

Your heart is like a diamond,
With such translucent light
That three times lucky is the man
On whom it shines tonight!

Your lips are like fine rubies,
Whose colour is so rare
That three times lucky is the man
Who kissed those lips so fair!

If ever I should find that man,
That thrice audacious lover,
Deep in a lonely woodland glade
His luck would soon be over!

– Heinrich Heine
  (translated from the German)

UNREQUITED LOVE

A young lad loves a maiden
Who would another wed;
The other loves another
And marries her instead.

The maiden weds in anger
The first and best young buck
Who comes her way thereafter;
The young lad rues his luck.

It is an age-old story,
Yet one that's ever new;
And every time it happens
A heart is rent in two.

– Heinrich Heine
  (translated from the German)

LORELEI

I know not why my mind is by
Such sombre thoughts beset;
A haunting tale from long ago
That I cannot forget.

The Rhine is calm as evening's shadows
Lengthen from the West;
The dying embers of the sun
Ignite the clifftop crest.

High on a rugged precipice
There sits a maiden fair;
Her golden jewels glisten
As she combs her golden hair.

She combs it with a golden comb
And sings a song withal,
A strangely lilting melody
That holds men in its thrall.

The boatman, in his fragile craft,
Entranced by thoughts of love,
Is heedless of the jutting rock –
He can but gaze above.

Methinks the waves will swallow up
Both man and boat ere long,
For surely has the Lorelei
Bewitched him with her song.

– Heinrich Heine
   (translated from the German)

TIME OF ROSES

It was not in the Winter
Our loving lot was cast;
It was the time of roses —
We pluck'd them as we pass'd!

That churlish season never frown'd
On early lovers yet:
O no — the world was newly crown'd
With flowers when first we met!

'Twas twilight, and I bade you go,
But still you held me fast;
It was the time of roses —
We pluck'd them as we pass'd!

– Thomas Hood (1799 - 1845)

RUTH

She stood breast high amid the corn,
Clasped by the golden light of morn,
Like the sweetheart of the sun,
Who many a glowing kiss had won.

On her cheek an autumn flush,
Deeply ripened; such a blush
In the midst of brown was born,
Like red poppies grown with corn.

Round her eyes her tresses fell,
Which were blackest none could tell,
But long lashes veiled a light,
That had else been all too bright.

And her hat, with shady brim,
Made her tressy forehead dim;
Thus she stood amid the stooks,
Praising God with sweetest looks:

Sure, I said, heaven did not mean,
Where I reap thou shouldst but glean,
Lay thy sheaf adown and come,
Share my harvest and my home.

– Thomas Hood

SERENADE

Through the darkness my entreaties
Wing their way to thee.
Down into this silent arbour
Come, my love, to me.

Slender treetops whisper softly
In the moonlit haze;
Lovely maiden, do not fear
The craven traitor's gaze.

Hear the sound of nightingales
Imploring tenderly,
With their songs of sweet lament
They send my prayers to thee.

They discern the bosom's yearning,
Know a lover's pain,
Touching every tender heart
With silver-sweet refrain.

May love's ardour fill thy breast,
My darling, hear my plea!
Trembling, I await our meeting —
Come, enrapture me!

– Ludwig Rellstab (1799 - 1860)
   (translated from the German)

THE JOURNEY

Tomorrow, when the dawn renders the landscape white,
I shall depart. I know you're waiting for me too.
I'll traverse wood and field, valley and mountainside.
No longer can I bear to be apart from you.

In silence I shall walk, my ears immune to sound,
My eyes fixed on my thoughts, oblivious to sight,
Alone, unrecognised, back bent toward the ground,
And daylight will to me be like the darkest night.

I shall not pause to gaze on evening's golden grace,
Nor watch the distant sails descending on Harfleur,
And then, when I arrive, upon your grave I'll place
A wreath of holly green and flowering heather there.

– Victor Hugo (1802 – 1885)
  (translated from the French)

If thou must love me, let it be for nought

If thou must love me, let it be for nought
Except for love's sake only. Do not say,
"I love her for her smile—her look—her way
Of speaking gently,—for a trick of thought
That falls in well with mine, and certes brought
A sense of pleasant ease on such a day"—
For these things in themselves, Belovèd, may
Be changed, or change for thee—and love, so wrought,
May be unwrought so. Neither love me for
Thine own dear pity's wiping my cheeks dry:
A creature might forget to weep, who bore
Thy comfort long, and lose thy love thereby!
But love me for love's sake, that evermore
Thou mayst love on, through love's eternity.

– Elizabeth Barrett Browning (1806 –1861)

How do I love thee? Let me count the ways.

How do I love thee? Let me count the ways.
I love thee to the depth and breadth and height
My soul can reach, when feeling out of sight
For the ends of being and ideal grace.
I love thee to the level of every day's
Most quiet need, by sun and candle-light.
I love thee freely, as men strive for right.
I love thee purely, as they turn from praise.
I love thee with the passion put to use
In my old griefs, and with my childhood's faith.
I love thee with a love I seemed to lose
With my lost saints. I love thee with the breath,
Smiles, tears, of all my life; and, if God choose,
I shall but love thee better after death.

– Elizabeth Barrett Browning

SONNET

My soul conceals a secret, my life a mystery;
A love born in an instant, ever to remain;
A love devoid of hope, a love that cannot be,
And she whom it concerns knows nothing of my pain.

Alas! She'll never know the longing that I feel.
Forever by her side, yet silent and alone,
I shall throughout my life be destined to conceal
This yearning for a heart I dare not make my own.

And she, whom God has made so gentle, sweet, and dear,
Will tread the path of life, never disposed to hear
That silent sigh of love that follows her always.

Piously devoted to life's austere command,
She'll say, hearing these verses singing in her praise:
"Who can this woman be?" and will not understand.

– Félix Arvers (1806 – 1850)
   (translated from the French)

Break, break, break ...

Break, break, break,
On thy cold grey stones, O Sea!
And I would that my tongue could utter
The thoughts that arise in me.

O, well for the fisherman's boy,
That he shouts with his sister at play!
O, well for the sailor lad,
That he sings in his boat on the bay!

And the stately ships go on
To their haven under the hill;
But O for the touch of a vanish'd hand,
And the sound of a voice that is still!

Break, break, break
At the foot of thy crags, O Sea!
But the tender grace of a day that is dead
Will never come back to me.

– Alfred, Lord Tennyson (1809 - 1892)

Go not, happy day...

Go not, happy day
From the shining fields,
Go not, happy day,
Till the maiden yields.
Rosy is the West,
Rosy is the South,
Roses are her cheeks,
And a rose her mouth.

When the happy Yes
Falters from her lips,
Pass and blush the news
Over glowing ships;
Over blowing seas,
Over seas at rest,
Pass the happy news,
Blush it thro' the West;

Till the red man dance
By his red cedar-tree,
And the red man's babe
Leap beyond the sea.

Blush from West to East,
Blush from East to West,
Till the West is East,
Blush it thro' the West.
Rosy is the West,
Rosy is the South,
Roses are her cheeks,
And a rose her mouth.

– Alfred, Lord Tennyson

Birds in the high hall garden...

Birds in the high hall garden
When twilight was falling,
Maud, Maud, Maud, Maud,
They were crying and calling.

Where was Maud? In our wood;
And I, who else? was with her,
Gathering woodland lilies,
Myriads blow together.

Birds in our wood sang,
Ringing thro' the valleys,
Maud is here, here, here
In among the lilies.

I kiss'd her slender hand,
She took the kiss sedately;
Maud is not seventeen,
But she is tall and stately.

I know the way she went
Home with her maiden posy,
For her feet have touch'd the meadows
And left the daisies rosy.

– Alfred, Lord Tennyson

Come into the garden, Maud...

Come into the garden, Maud,
For the black bat, Night, has flown,
Come into the garden, Maud,
I am here at the gate alone;
And the woodbine spices are wafted abroad,
And the musk of the roses blown.

For a breeze of morning moves,
And the planet of Love is on high,
Beginning to faint in the light that she loves
On a bed of daffodil sky,
To faint in the light of the sun she loves,
To faint in his light, and to die.

All night have the roses heard
The flute, violin, bassoon;
All night has the casement jessamine stirr'd
To the dancers dancing in tune:
Till a silence fell with the waking bird,
And a hush with the setting moon.

I said to the lily, "There is but one
With whom she has heart to be gay.
When will the dancers leave her alone?
She is weary of dance and play."
Now half to the setting moon are gone,
And half to the rising day;
Low on the sand and loud on the stone
The last wheel echoes away.

I said to the rose, "The brief night goes
In babble and revel and wine.
O young lordlover, what sighs are those
For one that will never be thine?
But mine, but mine," so I sware to the rose,
"For ever and ever, mine."

Come into the garden, Maud...

And the soul of the rose went into my blood,
As the music clash'd in the hall;
And long by the garden lake I stood,
For I heard your rivulet fall
From the lake to the meadow and on to the wood,
Our wood, that is dearer than all;

From the meadow your walks have left so sweet
That whenever a March-wind sighs
He sets the jewelprint of your feet
In violets blue as your eyes,
To the woody hollows in which we meet
And the valleys of Paradise.

The slender acacia would not shake
One long milk-bloom on the tree;
The white lake-blossom fell into the lake,
As the pimpernel dozed on the lea;
But the rose was awake all night for your sake,
Knowing your promise to me;
The lilies and roses were all awake,
They sigh'd for the dawn and thee.

Queen rose of the rosebud garden of girls,
Come hither, the dances are done,
In gloss of satin and glimmer of pearls,
Queen lily and rose in one;
Shine out, little head, sunning over with curls,
To the flowers, and be their sun.

There has fallen a splendid tear
From the passion-flower at the gate.
She is coming, my dove, my dear;
She is coming, my life, my fate;
The red rose cries, "She is near, she is near;"
And the white rose weeps, "She is late;"
The larkspur listens, "I hear, I hear;"
And the lily whispers, "I wait."

Come into the garden, Maud...

She is coming, my own, my sweet;
Were it ever so airy a tread,
My heart would hear her and beat,
Were it earth in an earthy bed;
My dust would hear her and beat,
Had I lain for a century dead;
Would start and tremble under her feet,
And blossom in purple and red.

– Alfred, Lord Tennyson

A DREAM WITHIN A DREAM

Take this kiss upon the brow!
And, in parting from you now,
Thus much let me avow--
You are not wrong, who deem
That my days have been a dream;
Yet if hope has flown away
In a night, or in a day,
In a vision, or in none,
Is it therefore the less gone?
All that we see or seem
Is but a dream within a dream.

I stand amid the roar
Of a surf-tormented shore,
And I hold within my hand
Grains of the golden sand--
How few! yet how they creep
Through my fingers to the deep,
While I weep--while I weep!
O God! can I not grasp
Them with a tighter clasp?
O God! can I not save
One from the pitiless wave?
Is all that we see or seem
But a dream within a dream?

– Edgar Allan Poe (1809 - 1849)

ANNABEL LEE

It was many and many a year ago,
In a kingdom by the sea,
That a maiden there lived whom you may know
By the name of Annabel Lee; —
And this maiden she lived with no other thought
Than to love and be loved by me.

She was a child and I was a child,
In this kingdom by the sea,
But we loved with a love that was more than love —
I and my Annabel Lee —
With a love that the winged seraphs of Heaven
Coveted her and me.

And this was the reason that, long ago,
In this kingdom by the sea,
A wind blew out of a cloud by night
Chilling my Annabel Lee;
So that her high-born kinsmen came
And bore her away from me,
To shut her up in a sepulchre
In this kingdom by the sea.

The angels, not half so happy in Heaven,
Went envying her and me: —
Yes! that was the reason (as all men know,
In this kingdom by the sea)
That the wind came out of the cloud, chilling
And killing my Annabel Lee.

But our love it was stronger by far than the love
Of those who were older than we —
Of many far wiser than we —
And neither the angels in Heaven above
Nor the demons down under the sea,
Can ever dissever my soul from the soul
Of the beautiful Annabel Lee: —

ANNABEL LEE

For the moon never beams without bringing me dreams
Of the beautiful Annabel Lee;
And the stars never rise but I see the bright eyes
Of the beautiful Annabel Lee;
And so, all the night-tide, I lie down by the side
Of my darling, my darling, my life and my bride
In the sepulchre there by the sea —
In her tomb by the side of the sea.

– Edgar Allan Poe

NOW

Out of your whole life give but a moment!
All of your life that has gone before,
All to come after it, - so you ignore,
So you make perfect the present, condense,
In a rapture of rage, for perfection's endowment,
Thought and feeling and soul and sense,
Merged in a moment which gives me at last
You around me for once, you beneath me, above me -
Me, sure that, despite of time future, time past,
This tick of life-time's one moment you love me!
How long such suspension may linger? Ah, Sweet,
The moment eternal - just that and no more -
When ecstasy's utmost we clutch at the core,
While cheeks burn, arms open, eyes shut, and lips meet!

– Robert Browning (1812 – 1889)

LIFE IN A LOVE

Escape me?
Never—
Beloved!
While I am I, and you are you,
So long as the world contains us both,
Me the loving and you the loth,
While the one eludes, must the other pursue.
My life is a fault at last, I fear:
It seems too much like a fate, indeed!
Though I do my best I shall scarce succeed.
But what if I fail of my purpose here?
It is but to keep the nerves at strain,
To dry one's eyes and laugh at a fall,
And, baffled, get up and begin again,—
So the chase takes up one's life, that's all.
While, look but once from your farthest bound
At me so deep in the dust and dark,
No sooner the old hope goes to ground
Than a new one, straight to the self-same mark,
I shape me—
Ever
Removed!

– Robert Browning

Sweet evenings come and go, love...

> "La noche buena se viene,
> La noche buena se va,
> Y nosotros nos iremos
> Y no volveremos mas."
> -- Old Villancico.

Sweet evenings come and go, love,
They came and went of yore:
This evening of our life, love,
Shall go and come no more.

When we have passed away, love,
All things will keep their name;
But yet no life on earth, love,
With ours will be the same.

The daisies will be there, love,
The stars in heaven will shine:
I shall not feel thy wish, love,
Nor thou my hand in thine.

A better time will come, love,
And better souls be born:
I would not be the best, love,
To leave thee now forlorn.

– George Eliot (1819 - 1880))

A FAREWELL

I

My fairest child, I have no song to give you;
No lark could pipe to skies so dull and grey:
Yet, ere we part, one lesson I can leave you
For every day.

II

Be good, sweet maid, and let who will be clever;
Do noble things, not dream them, all day long:
And so make life, death, and that vast for-ever
One grand, sweet song.

– Charles Kingsley (1819 - 1875)

YOUNG AND OLD

When all the world is young, lad,
And all the trees are green;
And every goose a swan, lad,
And every lass a queen;
Then hey for boot and horse, lad,
And round the world away!
Young blood must have its course, lad,
And every dog his day.

When all the world is old, lad,
And all the trees are brown;
And all the sport is stale, lad,
And all the wheels run down;
Creep home, and take your place there,
The spent and maimed among;
God grant you find one face there,
You loved when all was young.

– Charles Kingsley

TO A PASSER-BY

About me roared the noise and clamour of the town.
A widow, new-bereaved, tall, slender, stately, grand,
Passed by, and with a graceful gesture of her hand,
Lifted the scalloped border of her mourning gown.

Enchanted by her grace, her perfect symmetry,
Delirious, I drank, enraptured yet forlorn,
From her eyes, livid skies where hurricanes are born,
The sweetness that enthrals, the lethal ecstasy.

A lightning flash — then night! — O fugitive beauty,
Whose single passing glance kindled new life in me,
Shall I see you again but in eternity?

Elsewhere, so far from here! too late! *never*, maybe?
For I know not your fate, nor you my destiny,
You whom I might have loved, you knew it, fleetingly!

– Charles Baudelaire (1821 – 1867)
  (translated from the French)

THE FOUNTAIN

Your lovely eyes are tired, poor sweet!
Sleep on in that unstudied guise,
So nonchalantly indiscreet,
Where pleasure took you by surprise.
The fountain burbles endlessly
Out in the courtyard, day and night,
Sustaining the sweet ecstasy
That love accorded me tonight.

There blossoms forth a spray
Of floral spheres,
Where Phoebe's bright display
Gaily appears,
And falls in a cascade
Of heavy tears.

And thus your ardent soul ignites
In hedonistic ecstasy,
And rushes boldly to the heights
Of the vast sky's infinity,
Until, expiring, losing hope,
In languid dole it falls apart,
Cascading down a hidden slope
Into the haven of my heart.

There blossoms forth a spray
Of floral spheres,
Where Phoebe's bright display
Gaily appears,
And falls in a cascade
Of heavy tears.

THE FOUNTAIN

You whom the night doth render fair,
How sweet it is, upon your breast,
To hear, in the ethereal air,
The fountains sobbing without rest!
Moon, rippling water, blessed night,
Leaves whispering in the trees above,
The languor of your sweet delight
Is the reflection of my love.

There blossoms forth a spray
Of floral spheres,
Where Phoebe's bright display
Gaily appears,
And falls in a cascade
Of heavy tears.

– Charles Baudelaire
   (translated from the French)

INVITATION TO A JOURNEY

My sister, my heart,
How sweet to depart
To that faraway haven with you!
To languidly lie,
To love and to die
In a land that resembles you!
The damp suns that rise
In nebulous skies
Seem to mirror the charm that appears
In the mystic disguise
Of your treacherous eyes,
Glistening through their tears.

There, all is order and beauty,
Luxury, calm and ecstasy.

Furnishings fine,
Embellished by time,
Would decorate our room;
And flowers most rare
Their fragrance would share
With amber's heady perfume,
Ceilings ornate,
And walls with the weight
Of Orient's splendour hung,
All things there would speak
In the secret mystique
Of their gentle native tongue.

There, all is order and beauty,
Luxury, calm, and ecstasy.

INVITATION TO A JOURNEY

See the vessels that brave
The wind and the wave
Rocking gently in their berth;
It is to inspire
Your every desire
That they come from the ends of the earth.
— The sun goes down,
Setting the town,
The meadows and rivers alight
With jacinth and gold;
Our dreams unfold
In a gently warming light.

There, all is order and beauty,
Luxury, calm and ecstasy.

– Charles Baudelaire
 (translated from the French)

A HEMISPHERE IN YOUR HAIR

O tresses that enfold your shoulders with such grace!
O curls! O fragrance wafting nonchalantly there!
What rapture! And to fill the boudoir's sombre space
With memories that sleep in this luxuriant place,
I want to shake it like a kerchief in the air!

Asia, where languor dwells, Africa's scorching heat,
Those distant worlds, whose absent wonders are so rare,
Live in the depths of this ambrosial retreat!
While other spirits float on sounds of music sweet,
Mine, O my love! bathes in the perfume of your hair.

I'll go where trees and men live in serenity,
Beneath an ardent sun taking their languid ease.
Thick tresses, be the swell that lifts and carries me!
You hold, ebony sea, a dazzling reverie,
Of masts and sails afloat upon a zephyr breeze:

A busy haven where my spirit can inhale
A flood of sound and colour, fragrance, purity,
Where vessels glide on seas of amber in full sail,
Unfolding wide their arms to greet the majesty
Of a pure sky where warmth resides eternally.

And I shall plunge my head in eager drunkenness
Into this black sea where the other is enclosed,
And my keen spirit, that the gentle waves caress,
Will know where you reside, O fecund idleness,
Eternal lullaby of sweet-scented repose!

Enchanting locks, unfurling like a banner, where
I revel in the azure blue of skies afar;
In the abundant depths of this luxuriant hair
I ardently imbibe the mingled perfumes there,
The oil of coconut, the heady musk and tar.

A HEMISPHERE IN YOUR HAIR

Always! forever! in your flowing locks entwined,
My hand will sow pearls, rubies, sapphires crystalline,
So that to my desire you never will be blind!
Are you not the oasis where I dream, the vine
From which I take long draughts of your nostalgic wine?

– Charles Baudelaire
   (translated from the French)

THE POISON

Wine knows how to embellish the most sordid room
With a luxurious disguise,
Making the most fantastic colonnades arise
In the gold of its crimson bloom,
Like the sun's dying rays suffusing misty skies.

Opium magnifies that which is limitless,
Extends beyond infinity,
Amplifies time, intensifies cupidity,
And with thrills dark and joyless
Pervades the soul beyond its full capacity.

Yet neither can compete with the poison that flows
From your eyes, your green eyes so fair,
Lakes where my soul recoils from its reflection there...
My dreams have no repose
And to those bitter gulfs in multitudes repair.

There's nothing that can match the terrible prowess
Of your saliva and your breath,
Which cast into oblivion my soul without redress,
Depriving it of consciousness,
And pushing it, expiring, to the shores of death!

– Charles Baudelaire
  (translated from the French)

One night as I lay with a wanton hussy by my side

One night as I lay with a wanton hussy by my side,
Like a cadaver that a fellow corpse has sought,
I called to mind, beside that body I had bought,
The one for whom my love too long had been denied.

I saw in my mind's eye her native majesty,
Her candid gaze, so full of energy and grace,
Her hair, a perfumed hood that frames her lovely face,
Of which my heart retains the ardent memory.

For fain would I have kissed a body I revere,
And from your fragrant feet to your obsidian tresses,
Unleashed the treasury of my profound caresses,

If, one night, you could just have shed one artless tear,
O queen whose cruelty your beauty so belies,
To dull the splendour of your cold uncaring eyes.

– Charles Baudelaire
(translated from the French)

HYMN

To her most dear, to her most fair
Who fills my heart with clarity,
To an angel beyond compare,
Greetings in immortality!

She flows into my consciousness
Like a salt breeze's soft caress,
And into my unsated soul
She pours a taste of timelessness.

Ever fresh sachet that perfumes
A cherished place with sweet delight,
Forgotten incense bowl that fumes
In secrecy throughout the night,

How, love that's incorruptible,
Can I describe you truthfully?
A grain of musk, invisible,
Deep in my soul's eternity!

To her most dear, to her most fair,
My joy and my felicity,
To an angel beyond compare,
Greetings in immortality!

– Charles Baudelaire
   (translated from the French)

A PERFECT WHOLE

The Devil came to call on me
This morning in my attic room,
And, seeking to befuddle me,
Said: "Tell me, if I may presume,

Among the wonders that compose
The beauty of her form so fair,
Among the objects, black or rose,
That lend her such a charming air,

Which is the sweetest?" — O my Soul!
You did reply to the Abhorred:
"In truth, she is a perfect whole:
Each virtue brings its own reward.

Her every feature gives delight —
What charms me most? I do not know.
She is the solace of the Night,
The radiance of Aurora's glow.

A most exquisite harmony
Pervades the union of her arts,
And no impotent scrutiny
Can separate the diverse parts.

O mystic metamorphosis
Of every sense uniquely blent!
Her breath is music's synthesis,
And her voice gives forth fragrant scent!"

– Charles Baudelaire
   (translated from the French)

THE PORTRAIT

Disease and Death reduce to ash and cinder
Our passion that once burned with ardent fire.
Of those wide eyes so fervent and so tender,
That mouth where my heart drowned in deep desire,

Of those clandestine kisses that we stole,
Those transports more intense than lambent rays,
What now remains? It's awful, O my soul!
Just a three-coloured sketch, a pallid haze,

Which, like me, dies and slowly fades away,
And which harsh Time, malignant patriarch,
Abrades with his rough pinion every day...

Killer of Life and Art, assassin dark,
You'll never banish from my memory
The one who was my joy and majesty!

– Charles Baudelaire
   (translated from the French)

THE BALCONY

Mother of memories, mistress of mistresses,
O you my every bliss! O you my every duty!
You will recall the joy of our profound caresses,
The comfort of the hearth, the evening's tranquil beauty,
Mother of memories, mistress of mistresses!

The evenings by the fire, lit by the burning coal,
And on the balcony, veiled in a rosy hue,
The softness of your breast, the sweetness of your soul!
We said so many things that were forever true,
The evenings by the fire, lit by the burning coal!

How beautiful the sunlight on a summer's night!
How deep the vault of heaven! How strong the beating heart!
Holding you close to me, O queen of my delight,
It seemed your very blood did its sweet scent impart.
How beautiful the sunlight on a summer's night!

The wall of darkness thickened, shutting out the light,
And in the gloom my eyes sought your eyes longingly,
And I imbibed your breath, O poisonous delight!
And in my loving hands your feet slept peacefully.
The wall of darkness thickened, shutting out the light.

The recollection of sweet moments is an art
That lets me live again those hours of happiness.
Why should I seek elsewhere than in your loving heart,
And in your gracious form, the joys of languidness?
The recollection of sweet moments is an art!

Those vows, those fragrant scents, those kisses without end,
Can they be born again from gulfs we cannot sound,
Just as the endless seas back to the heavens send
Rejuvenated suns that from their depths rebound?
— O vows! O fragrant scents! O kisses without end!

- Charles Baudelaire
  (translated from the French)

THE LOVERS' WINE

How splendid is the world today!
Without bit or spur, lets away
Upon our mounts of heady wine
To heavens magic and divine!

Like two angels tormented by
An ardent flame that will not die,
In the bright morning's crystal blue
Let us the far mirage pursue.

Riding and rocking languidly
On an all-knowing, swirling tide,
In a parallel ecstasy,

My sister, floating side by side,
We'll follow these exotic streams
To the nirvana of my dreams!

– Charles Baudelaire
 (translated from the French)

THE LOVERS' DEATH

We shall have beds imbued with subtle scents,
And ottomans as deep as any tomb,
And flow'rs of mystic fragrance redolent
That under fairer skies for us will bloom.

Burning ever more ardent and more bright,
Our hearts will shine like beacons from above,
Each sending forth its pure reflected light
To the twin mirrors of our endless love.

One evening made of rose and mystic blue,
We shall exchange an ultimate adieu,
A last scintilla of this earthly life;

And later an Angelic form will pass,
To faithfully and joyously revive
The dormant embers and the tarnished glass.

– Charles Baudelaire
   (translated from the French)

LONGING

Come to me in my dreams, and then
By day I shall be well again.
For then the night will more than pay
The hopeless longing of the day.

Come, as thou cam'st a thousand times,
A messenger from radiant climes,
And smile on thy new world, and be
As kind to others as to me.

Or, as thou never cam'st in sooth,
Come now, and let me dream it truth.
And part my hair, and kiss my brow,
And say My love! why sufferest thou?

Come to me in my dreams, and then
By day I shall be well again.
For then the night will more than pay
The hopeless longing of the day.

– Matthew Arnold (1822 – 1888)

BEAUTIFUL DREAMER

Beautiful dreamer, wake unto me,
Starlight and dewdrops are waiting for thee;
Sounds of the rude world heard in the day,
Lull'd by the moonlight have all pass'd away!

Beautiful dreamer, queen of my song,
List while I woo thee with soft melody;
Gone are the cares of life's busy throng, —
Beautiful dreamer, awake unto me!

Beautiful dreamer, out on the sea
Mermaids are chaunting the wild lorelie;
Over the streamlet vapors are borne,
Waiting to fade at the bright coming morn.

Beautiful dreamer, beam on my heart,
E'en as the morn on the streamlet and sea;
Then will all clouds of sorrow depart, —
Beautiful dreamer, awake unto me!

– Stephen Foster (1826 –1864)

JEANIE WITH THE LIGHT BROWN HAIR

I dream of Jeanie with the light brown hair,
Borne, like a vapor on the summer air;
I see her playing where the bright streams play,
Happy as the daisies that dance on her way.
Many were the wild notes her merry voice would pour.
Many were the blithe birds that warbled them o'er:
Oh, I dream of Jeanie with the light brown hair,
Floating, like a vapor, on the soft summer air.

I long for Jeanie with a day-dawn smile,
Radiant in gladness, warm with winning guile;
I hear her melodies, like joys gone by,
Sighing round my heart over the fond hopes that die:
Sighing like the night wind and sobbing like the rain,
Wailing for the lost one that comes not again:
Oh, I long for Jeanie, and my heart bows low,
Never more to find her where the bright waters flow.

I sigh for Jeanie, but her light form strayed
Far from the fond hearts round her native glade;
Her smiles have vanished and her sweet songs flown,
Flitting like the dreams that have cheered us and gone.
Now the nodding wild flowers may wither on the shore
While her gentle fingers will cull them no more:
Oh, I sigh for Jeanie with the light brown hair,
Floating, like a vapor, on the soft summer air.

– Stephen Foster

REMEMBER

Remember me when I am gone away,
Gone far away into the silent land;
When you can no more hold me by the hand,
Nor I half turn to go yet turning stay.
Remember me when no more day by day
You tell me of our future that you plann'd:
Only remember me; you understand
It will be late to counsel then or pray.
Yet if you should forget me for a while
And afterwards remember, do not grieve:
For if the darkness and corruption leave
A vestige of the thoughts that once I had,
Better by far you should forget and smile
Than that you should remember and be sad.

– Christina Rossetti (1830 - 1894)

I loved you first...

I loved you first: but afterwards your love
Outsoaring mine, sang such a loftier song
As drowned the friendly cooings of my dove.
Which owes the other most? my love was long,
And yours one moment seemed to wax more strong;
I loved and guessed at you, you construed me
And loved me for what might or might not be –
Nay, weights and measures do us both a wrong.
For verily love knows not 'mine' or 'thine;'
With separate 'I' and 'thou' free love has done,
For one is both and both are one in love:
Rich love knows nought of 'thine that is not mine;'
Both have the strength and both the length thereof,
Both of us, of the love which makes us one.

– Christina Rossetti

THE FIRST DAY

I wish I could remember the first day,
First hour, first moment of your meeting me;
If bright or dim the season it might be;
Summer or winter for aught I can say.
So, unrecorded did it slip away,
So blind was I to see and to foresee,
So dull to mark the budding of my tree
That would not blossom, yet, for many a May.
If only I could recollect it! Such
A day of days! I let it come and go
As traceless as a thaw of bygone snow.
It seemed to mean so little, meant so much!
If only now I could recall that touch,
First touch of hand in hand! - Did one but know!

– Christina Rossetti

Somewhere or other...

Somewhere or other there must surely be
The face not seen, the voice not heard,
The heart that not yet — never yet — ah me!
Made answer to my word.

Somewhere or other, may be near or far;
Past land and sea, clean out of sight;
Beyond the wandering moon, beyond the star
That tracks her night by night.

Somewhere or other, may be far or near;
With just a wall, a hedge, between;
With just the last leaves of the dying year
Fallen on a turf grown green.

– Christina Rossetti

ECHO

Come to me in the silence of the night;
Come in the sparkling silence of a dream;
Come with soft rounded cheeks and eyes as bright
As sunlight on a stream;
Come back in tears,
O memory, hope, love of finished years.

O dream how sweet, too sweet, too bitter sweet,
Whose wakening should have been in Paradise,
Where souls brim-full of love abide and meet;
Where thirsting longing eyes
Watch the slow door
That opening, letting in, lets out no more.

Yet come to me in dreams, that I may live
My very life again though cold in death:
Come back to me in dreams, that I may give
Pulse for pulse, breath for breath:
Speak low, lean low,
As long ago, my love, how long ago.

– Christina Rossetti

A charm invests a face...

A charm invests a face
Imperfectly beheld.
The lady dare not lift her veil
For fear it be dispelled.

But peers beyond her mesh,
And wishes, and denies,
Lest interview annul a want
That image satisfies.

– Emily Dickinson (1830 – 1886)

That I did always love

That I did always love
I bring thee Proof
That till I loved
I never lived — Enough —

That I shall love alway —
I argue thee
That love is life —
And life hath Immortality —

This — dost thou doubt — Sweet —
Then have I
Nothing to show
But Calvary —

- Emily Dickinson

For each ecstatic instant...

For each ecstatic instant
We must an anguish pay.
In keen and quivering ratio
To the ecstasy.

For each beloved hour
Sharp pittances of years,
Bitter contested farthings
And coffers heaped with tears.

– Emily Dickinson

You left me, sweet...

You left me, sweet, two legacies, -
A legacy of love
A Heavenly Father would content,
Had He the offer of;

You left me boundaries of pain
Capacious as the sea,
Between eternity and time,
Your consciousness and me.

– Emily Dickinson

Wild nights - Wild nights!

Wild nights - Wild nights!
Were I with thee
Wild nights should be
Our luxury!

Futile - the winds -
To a Heart in port -
Done with the Compass -
Done with the Chart!

Rowing in Eden -
Ah - the Sea!
Might I but moor - tonight -
In thee!

– Emily Dickinson

If you were coming in the fall...

If you were coming in the fall
I'd brush the summer by
With half a smile and half a spurn
As housewives do a fly.

If I could see you in a year
I'd wind the months in balls
And put them into separate drawers
Until their time befalls.

If only centuries delayed
I'd count them on my hand
Subtracting 'till my fingers dropped
Into Van Diemen's land.

If certain when this life was out
That yours and mine should be
I'd toss life yonder like a rind
And taste eternity.

But now all ignorant of length,
Of times uncertain wing,
It goads me like the goblin bee
That will not state its sting!

– Emily Dickinson

AT LAST

At last, when all the summer shine
That warmed life's early hours is past,
Your loving fingers seek for mine
And hold them close—-at last—-at last!
Not oft the robin comes to build
Its nest upon the leafless bough
By autumn robbed, by winter chilled, —-
But you, dear heart, you love me now.

Though there are shadows on my brow
And furrows on my cheek, in truth, —-
The marks where Time's remorseless plough
Broke up the blooming sward of Youth, —-
Though fled is every girlish grace
Might win or hold a lover's vow,
Despite my sad and faded face,
And darkened heart, you love me now!

I count no more my wasted tears;
They left no echo of their fall;
I mourn no more my lonesome years;
This blessed hour atones for all.
I fear not all that Time or Fate
May bring to burden heart or brow, —
Strong in the love that came so late,
Our souls shall keep it always now!

– Elizabeth Akers Allen (1832 – 1911)

LOVE IS ENOUGH

Love is enough: though the World be a-waning,
And the woods have no voice but the voice of complaining,
Though the sky be too dark for dim eyes to discover
The gold-cups and daisies fair blooming thereunder,
Though the hills be held shadows, and the sea a dark wonder
And this day draw a veil over all deeds pass'd over,
Yet their hands shall not tremble, their feet shall not falter;
The void shall not weary, the fear shall not alter
These lips and these eyes of the loved and the lover.

– William Morris (1834 – 1896)

LOVE'S TRINITY

Soul, heart, and body, we thus singly name,
Are not in love divisible and distinct,
But each with each inseparably link'd.
One is not honour, and the other shame,
But burn as closely fused as fuel, heat, and flame.

They do not love who give the body and keep
The heart ungiven; nor they who yield the soul,
And guard the body. Love doth give the whole;
Its range being high as heaven, as ocean deep,
Wide as the realms of air or planet's curving sweep.

– Alfred Austin (1835 – 1913)

FLORENTINE SERENADE

O star, whose pure transparent light
Shines like a diamond in the night,
Look down upon my love's repose
As her eyes now in slumber close.

Bestow on those beloved eyes
The benediction of the skies,
And, as she sleeps, her room infuse
With light from thy celestial muse.

Upon her whiteness let a strain
Of thy pure light till dawn remain,
And may she dream that up above
There rose a nascent star of love.

– Henri Cazalis (1840 – 1909)
   (translated from the French)

THE ANTIDOTE

In your heart sleeps a pale moonlight,
A gentle summer's evening,
And from life's turmoil taking flight
I shall immerse myself therein.

Past sorrows from my soul shall flee,
My darling, when your arms enlace
My troubled thoughts and aching heart
Within the calm of your embrace.

You'll cool the fever of my brow
With soft caresses from above,
And you will sing a ballad song
That tells the story of our love;

And in the haven of your eyes,
Sad eyes that understand my pain,
I shall imbibe such tenderness
That I shall be made well again.

– Henri Cazalis
   (translated from the French)

NEUTRAL TONES

We stood by a pond that winter day,
And the sun was white, as though chidden of God,
And a few leaves lay on the starving sod;
– They had fallen from an ash, and were grey.

Your eyes on me were as eyes that rove
Over tedious riddles of years ago;
And some words played between us to and fro
On which lost the more by our love.

The smile on your mouth was the deadest thing
Alive enough to have strength to die;
And a grin of bitterness swept thereby
Like an ominous bird a-wing....

Since then, keen lessons that love deceives,
And wrings with wrong, have shaped to me
Your face, and the God curst sun, and a tree,
And a pond edged with greyish leaves.

– Thomas Hardy (1840 – 1928)

THE VOICE

Woman much missed, how you call to me, call to me,
Saying that now you are not as you were
When you had changed from the one who was all to me,
But as at first, when our day was fair.
Can it be you that I hear? Let me view you, then,
Standing as when I drew near to the town
Where you would wait for me: yes, as I knew you then,
Even to the original air-blue gown!

Or is it only the breeze in its listlessness
Travelling across the wet mead to me here,
You being ever dissolved to wan wistlessness,
Heard no more again far or near?

Thus I; faltering forward,
Leaves around me falling,
Wind oozing thin through the thorn from norward,
And the woman calling.

– Thomas Hardy

MY FAMILIAR DREAM

I often have this strange and penetrating dream
About a woman, whom I love and who loves me,
And who, each time I dream, is never quite the same,
Nor is she yet another, and loves and understands me.

For she can understand me, and my heart that's clear
For her alone, alas, is not a problem now
For her, and the moist droplets of my pallid brow,
She only has the power to cool them with a tear.

Is her hair auburn, dark, or fair? - I do not know.
Her name? as I recall, its gentle accents flow
In names of those we loved, now banished from this life.

Her gaze is reminiscent of a statue's gaze,
And her voice, distant, calm and grave, reminds me of
The voices that I knew and loved in bygone days.

– Paul Verlaine (1844 – 1896)
   (translated from the French)

My delight and thy delight…

My delight and thy delight
Walking, like two angels white,
In the gardens of the night:

My desire and thy desire
Twining to a tongue of fire,
Leaping live, and laughing higher:

Thro' the everlasting strife
In the mystery of life.

Love, from whom the world begun,
Hath the secret of the sun.

Love can tell, and love alone,
Whence the million stars were strewn,
Why each atom knows its own,
How, in spite of woe and death,
Gay is life, and sweet is breath:

This he taught us, this we knew,
Happy in his science true,
Hand in hand as we stood
'Neath the shadows of the wood,
Heart to heart as we lay
In the dawning of the day.

– Robert Seymour Bridges (1844 – 1930)

So sweet love seemed that April morn...

So sweet love seemed that April morn,
When first we kissed beside the thorn,
So strangely sweet, it was not strange
We thought that love could never change.

But I can tell—let truth be told—
That love will change in growing old;
Though day by day is naught to see,
So delicate his motions be.

And in the end 'twill come to pass
Quite to forget what once he was,
Nor even in fancy to recall
The pleasure that was all in all.

His little spring, that sweet we found,
So deep in summer floods is drowned,
I wonder, bathed in joy complete,
How love so young could be so sweet.

– Robert Seymour Bridges

I WILL NOT LET THEE GO

I will not let thee go.
Ends all our month-long love in this?
Can it be summed up so,
Quit in a single kiss?
I will not let thee go.

I will not let thee go.
If thy words' breath could scare thy deeds,
As the soft south can blow
And toss the feathered seeds,
Then might I let thee go.

I will not let thee go.
Had not the great sun seen, I might;
Or were he reckoned slow
To bring the false to light,
Then might I let thee go.

I will not let thee go.
The stars that crowd the summer skies
Have watched us so below
With all their million eyes,
I dare not let thee go.

I will not let thee go.
Have we chid the changeful moon,
Now rising late, and now
Because she set too soon,
And shall I let thee go?

I will not let thee go.
Have not the young flowers been content,
Plucked ere their buds could blow,
To seal our sacrament?
I cannot let thee go.

I WILL NOT LET THEE GO

I will not let thee go.
I hold thee by too many bands:
Thou sayest farewell, and lo!
I have thee by the hands,
And will not let thee go.

– Robert Seymour Bridges

WHEN LOVE IS LOST

When love is lost, day sets toward the night,
Albeit the morning sun may still be bright,
And not one cloud-ship sails across the sky.
Yet from the places where it used to lie
Gone is the lustrous glory of the light.

No splendour rests in any mountain height,
No scene spreads fair and beauteous to the sight;
All, all seems dull and dreary to the eye
When love is lost.

Love lends to life its grandeur and its might;
Love goes, and leaves behind it gloom and blight;
Like ghosts of time the pallid hours drag by,
And grief's one happy thought is that we die.
Ah, what can recompense us for its flight
When love is lost?

– Ella Wheeler Wilcox (1850 – 1919)

LOVE'S COMING

She had looked for his coming as warriors come,
With the clash of arms and the bugle's call;
But he came instead with a stealthy tread,
Which she did not hear at all.

She had thought how his armor would blaze in the sun,
As he rode like a prince to claim his bride:
In the sweet dim light of the falling night
She found him at her side.

She had dreamed how the gaze of his strange, bold eye
Would wake her heart to a sudden glow:
She found in his face the familiar grace
Of a friend she used to know.

She had dreamed how his coming would stir her soul,
As the ocean is stirred by the wild storm's strife:
He brought her the balm of a heavenly calm,
And a peace which crowned her life.

– Ella Wheeler Wilcox

YOU WILL FORGET ME

You will forget me. The years are so tender,
They bind up the wounds which we think are so deep,
This dream of our youth will fade out as the splendour
Fades from the skies when the sun sinks to sleep,
The cloud of forgetfulness, over and over
Will banish the last rosy colours away,
And the fingers of time will weave garlands to cover
The scar which you think is a life-mark today.

You will forget me. The one boon you covet
Now above all things will soon. seem no prize,
And the heart, which you hold not in keeping to prove it
True or untrue, will lose worth in your eyes.
The one drop to-day, that you deem only wanting
To fill your life-cup to the brim, soon will seem
But a valueless mite; and the ghost that is haunting
The aisles of your heart will pass out with the dream.

You will forget me, will thank me for saying
The words which you think are so pointed with pain.
Time loves a new lay, and the dirge he is playing
Will change for you soon to a livelier strain.
I shall pass from your life, I shall pass out forever,
And these hours we have spent will be sunk in the past.
Youth buries its dead, grief kills seldom or never
And forgetfulness covers all sorrows at last.

– Ella Wheeler Wilcox

LOVE'S LANGUAGE

How does Love speak?
In the faint flush upon the telltale cheek,
And in the pallor that succeeds it; by
The quivering lid of an averted eye--
The smile that proves the parent to a sigh
Thus doth Love speak.

How does Love speak?
By the uneven heart-throbs, and the freak
Of bounding pulses that stand still and ache,
While new emotions, like strange barges, make
Along vein-channels their disturbing course;
Still as the dawn, and with the dawn's swift force--
Thus doth Love speak.

How does Love speak?
In the avoidance of that which we seek--
The sudden silence and reserve when near--
The eye that glistens with an unshed tear--
The joy that seems the counterpart of fear,
As the alarmed heart leaps in the breast,
And knows, and names, and greets its godlike guest-
Thus doth Love speak.

How does Love speak?
In the proud spirit suddenly grown meek--
The haughty heart grown humble; in the tender
And unnamed light that floods the world with splendor;
In the resemblance which the fond eyes trace
In all fair things to one beloved face;
In the shy touch of hands that thrill and tremble;
In looks and lips that can no more dissemble--
Thus doth Love speak.

LOVE'S LANGUAGE

How does Love speak?
In the wild words that uttered seem so weak
They shrink ashamed in silence; in the fire
Glance strikes with glance, swift flashing high and higher,
Like lightnings that precede the mighty storm;
In the deep, soulful stillness; in the warm,
Impassioned tide that sweeps through throbbing veins,
Between the shores of keen delights and pains;
In the embrace where madness melts in bliss,
And in the convulsive rapture of a kiss--
Thus doth Love speak.

– Ella Wheeler Wilcox

I LOVE YOU

I love your lips when they're wet with wine
    And red with a wild desire;
I love your eyes when the lovelight lies
    Lit with a passionate fire.
I love your arms when the warm white flesh
    Touches mine in a fond embrace;
I love your hair when the strands enmesh
    Your kisses against my face.

Not for me the cold, calm kiss
    Of a virgin's bloodless love;
Not for me the saint's white bliss,
    Nor the heart of a spotless dove.
But give me the love that so freely gives
    And laughs at the whole world's blame,
With your body so young and warm in my arms,
    It sets my poor heart aflame.

So kiss me sweet with your warm wet mouth,
    Still fragrant with ruby wine,
And say with a fervor born of the South
    That your body and soul are mine.
Clasp me close in your warm young arms,
    While the pale stars shine above,
And we'll live our whole young lives away
    In the joys of a living love.

– Ella Wheeler Wilcox

TO MY WIFE

I can write no stately poem
As a prelude to my lay;
From a poet to a poem
I would dare to say.
For if of these fallen petals
One to you seem fair,
Love will waft it till it settles
On your hair.
And when wind and winter harden
All the loveless land,
It will whisper of the garden,
You will understand.

And there is nothing left to do
But to kiss once again, and part,
Nay, there is nothing we should rue,
I have my beauty,-you your Art,
Nay, do not start,
One world was not enough for two
Like me and you.

– Oscar Wilde (1854 –1900)

A TRAGEDY

Among his books he sits all day
To think and read and write;
He does not smell the new-mown hay,
The roses red and white.

I walk among them all alone,
His silly, stupid wife;
The world seems tasteless, dead and done —
An empty thing is life.

At night his window casts a square
Of light upon the lawn;
I sometimes walk and watch it there
Until the chill of dawn.

I have no brain to understand
The books he loves to read;
I only have a heart and hand
He does not seem to need.

He calls me "Child" — lays on my hair
Thin fingers, cold and mild;
Oh! God of Love, who answers prayer,
I wish I were a child!

And no one sees and no one knows
(He least would know or see),
That ere Love gathers next year's rose
Death will have gathered me.

– Edith Nesbitt (1858 - 1924)

When the lad for longing sighs...

When the lad for longing sighs,
Mute and dull of cheer and pale,
If at death's own door he lies,
Maiden, you can heal his ail.

Lovers' ills are all to buy:
The wan look, the hollow tone,
The hung head, the sunken eye,
You can have them for your own.

Buy them, buy them: even and morn
Lovers' ills are all to sell,
Then you can lie down forlorn;
But the lover will be well.

– A. E. Housman (1859 – 1936)

Oh, when I was in love with you...

Oh, when I was in love with you
Then I was clean and brave,
And miles around the wonder grew
How well did I behave.

And now the fancy passes by
And nothing will remain,
And miles around they'll say that I
Am quite myself again.

– A. E. Housman

When I was one-and-twenty...

When I was one-and-twenty
I heard a wise man say,
"Give crowns and pounds and guineas
But not your heart away;
Give pearls away and rubies
But keep your fancy free."
But I was one-and-twenty,
No use to talk to me.

When I was one-and-twenty
I heard him say again,
"The heart out of the bosom
Was never given in vain;
'Tis paid with sighs a plenty
And sold for endless rue."
And I am two-and-twenty,
And oh, 'tis true, 'tis true.

– A. E. Housman

SILENT WORSHIP

Did you not hear my Lady
Go down the garden singing?
Blackbird and thrush were silent
To hear the alleys ringing.

Oh, saw you not my Lady
Out in the garden there,
Shaming the rose and lily,
For she is twice as fair.

Though I am nothing to her,
Though she must rarely look at me,
And though I could never woo her,
I love her till I die.

Surely you heard my Lady
Go down the garden singing,
Silencing all the songbirds
And setting the alleys ringing...

But surely you saw my Lady
Out in the garden there,
Rivalling the glittering sunshine
With a glory of golden hair.

– Sir Arthur Somervell (1863 –1937)

When you are old and grey...

When you are old and grey and full of sleep,
And, nodding by the fire, take down this book,
And slowly read, and dream of the soft look
Your eyes had once, and of their shadows deep.

How many loved your moments of glad grace
And loved your beauty with love false or true,
But one man loved the pilgrim soul in you,
And loved the sorrows of your changing face.

And bending down beside the glowing bars,
Murmur, a little sadly, how Love fled
And paced upon the mountain overhead
And hid his face amid a crowd of stars.

– William Butler Yeats (1865 – 1939)
(cf. *Sonnet for Helen*, page 17)

THE CLOTHS OF HEAVEN

Had I the heavens' embroidered cloths,
Enwrought with golden and silver light,
The blue and the dim and the dark cloths
Of night and light and the half-light,
I would spread the cloths under your feet:
But I, being poor, have only my dreams;
I have spread my dreams under your feet;
Tread softly because you tread on my dreams.

– William Butler Yeats

DOWN BY THE SALLEY GARDENS

Down by the Salley Gardens
My love and I did meet;
She passed the Salley Gardens
With little snow-white feet.
She bid me take love easy,
As the leaves grow on the tree;
But I, being young and foolish,
With her would not agree.

In a field by the river
My love and I did stand,
And on my leaning shoulder
She laid her snow-white hand.
She bid me take life easy,
As the grass grows on the weirs;
But I was young and foolish,
And now am full of tears.

– William Butler Yeats

NEVER GIVE ALL THE HEART

Never give all the heart, for love
Will hardly seem worth thinking of
To passionate women if it seem
Certain, and they never dream
That it fades out from kiss to kiss;
For everything that's lovely is
But a brief, dreamy, kind delight.
O never give the heart outright,
For they, for all smooth lips can say,
Have given their hearts up to the play.
And who could play it well enough
If deaf and dumb and blind with love?
He that made this knows all the cost,
For he gave all his heart and lost.

– William Butler Yeats

THE MIRABEAU BRIDGE

Beneath the Mirabeau Bridge flows the Seine
And our amours
Must I remember them
The joy would always come after the pain

Toll the midnight bell again
Days depart I remain

Hands entwined we idly passed our days
While underneath
The arms of our embrace
Flowed waters weary of our endless gaze

Toll the midnight bell again
Days depart I remain

Love flows away just as these waters flow
Love flows away
O how this life is slow
And how our hopes conspire to lay us low

Toll the midnight bell again
Days depart I remain

The days pass by in time's relentless flow
Neither past time
Nor love can ever now
Return beneath the Bridge of Mirabeau

Toll the midnight bell again
Days depart I remain

– Guillaume Apollinaire (1880 – 1918)
  (translated from the French)

LOVE ONE ANOTHER

Love one another, but make not a bond of love.

Let it rather be a moving sea between the shores of your souls.

Fill each other's cup, but drink not from one cup.

Give one another of your bread, but eat not from the same loaf.

Sing and dance together and be joyous, but let each one of you be alone.

Even as the strings of a lute are alone though they quiver with the same music.

Give your hearts, but not into each other's keeping.

For only the hand of life can contain your hearts.

And stand together, yet not too near together.

For the pillars of the temple stand apart.

And the oak tree and the cypress grow not in each other's shadow.

– Khalil Gibran (1883 –1931)

OF LOVE

They said to him "Speak to us of Love."

He looked upon the people, and there fell a stillness upon them. And with a great voice he said:

When love beckons to you, follow him, Though his ways are hard and steep. And when his wings enfold you yield to him, Though the sword hidden among his feathers may wound you. And when he speaks to you believe in him, Though his voice may shatter your dreams.

For even as love crowns you so shall he crucify you. Even as he is for your growth so he is for your pruning.

Even as he ascends to your height and caresses your tenderest branches, So shall he descend to your roots and shake them in their clinging to the earth.

All these things shall love do unto you that you may know the secrets of your heart, and in that knowledge become a fragment of Life's heart.

But if in your fear you would seek only love's peace and love's pleasure, Then it is better for you to cover yourself and pass out of love's door, Into the seasonless world where you shall laugh, but not all of your laughter, and weep, but not all of your tears.

Love gives nothing but itself and takes nothing but from itself. Love possesses not nor would it be possessed; For love is sufficient unto love.

When you love you should not say, "God is in my heart," but rather, "I am in the heart of God."

And think not you can direct the course of love, for love, if it finds you worthy, directs your course. Love has no other desire but to fulfil itself.

– Khalil Gibran

LET THESE BE YOUR DESIRES

Love has no other desire but to fulfil itself,
But if you love and must needs have desires,
Let these be your desires:

To melt and be like a running brook
That sings its melody to the night.
To know the pain of too much tenderness.
To be wounded by your own understanding of love;
And to bleed willingly and joyfully.
To wake at dawn with a winged heart
And give thanks for another day of loving;
To rest at the noon hour and meditate love's ecstasy;
To return home at eventide with gratitude;
And then to sleep with a prayer
For the beloved in your heart
And a song of praise upon your lips.

– Khalil Gibran

THE KISS

I hoped that he would love me,
And he has kissed my mouth,
But I am like a stricken bird
That cannot reach the south.

For though I know he loves me,
To-night my heart is sad;
His kiss was not so wonderful
As all the dreams I had.

– Sara Teasdale (1884 – 1933)

I am not yours…

I am not yours, not lost in you,
Not lost, although I long to be
Lost as a candle lit at noon,
Lost as a snowflake in the sea.

You love me, and I find you still
A spirit beautiful and bright,
Yet I am I, who long to be
Lost as a light is lost in light.

Oh plunge me deep in love - put out
My senses, leave me deaf and blind,
Swept by the tempest of your love,
A taper in a rushing wind.

– Sara Teasdale

ALONE

I am alone, in spite of love,
In spite of all I take and give —
In spite of all your tenderness,
Sometimes I am not glad to live.

I am alone, as though I stood
On the highest peak of the tired gray world,
About me only swirling snow,
Above me, endless space unfurled;

With earth hidden and heaven hidden,
And only my own spirit's pride
To keep me from the peace of those
Who are not lonely, having died.

– Sara Teasdale

I SHALL NOT CARE

When I am dead and over me bright April
Shakes out her rain-drenched hair,
Tho' you should lean above me broken-hearted,
I shall not care.

I shall have peace, as leafy trees are peaceful
When rain bends down the bough,
And I shall be more silent and cold-hearted
Than you are now.

– Sara Teasdale

AFTER LOVE

There is no magic any more,
We meet as other people do,
You work no miracle for me
Nor I for you.

You were the wind and I the sea —
There is no splendor any more,
I have grown listless as the pool
Beside the shore.

But though the pool is safe from storm
And from the tide has found surcease,
It grows more bitter than the sea,
For all its peace.

– Sara Teasdale

LOVE

Love is a breach in the walls, a broken gate,
Where that comes in that shall not go again;
Love sells the proud heart's citadel to Fate.
They have known shame, who love unloved. Even then,
When two mouths, thirsty each for each, find slaking,
And agony's forgot, and hushed the crying
Of credulous hearts, in heaven -- such are but taking
Their own poor dreams within their arms, and lying
Each in his lonely night, each with a ghost.
Some share that night. But they know love grows colder,
Grows false and dull, that was sweet lies at most.
Astonishment is no more in hand or shoulder,
But darkens, and dies out from kiss to kiss.
All this is love; and all love is but this.

– Rupert Brooke (1887 - 1915)

BEAUTY AND BEAUTY

When Beauty and Beauty meet
All naked, fair to fair,
The earth is crying-sweet,
And scattering-bright the air,
Eddying, dizzying, closing round,
With soft and drunken laughter;
Veiling all that may befall
After -- after --

Where Beauty and Beauty met,
Earth's still a-tremble there,
And winds are scented yet,
And memory-soft the air,
Bosoming, folding glints of light,
And shreds of shadowy laughter;
Not the tears that fill the years
After -- after –

– Rupert Brooke

I think I should have loved you presently...

I think I should have loved you presently,
And given in earnest words I flung in jest;
And lifted honest eyes for you to see,
And caught your hand against my cheek and breast;
And all my pretty follies flung aside
That won you to me, and beneath your gaze,
Naked of reticence and shorn of pride,
Spread like a chart my little wicked ways.
I, that had been to you, had you remained,
But one more waking from a recurrent dream,
Cherish no less the certain stakes I gained,
And walk your memory's halls, austere, supreme,
A ghost in marble of a girl you knew
Who would have loved you in a day or two.

– Edna St. Vincent Millay (1892 – 1950)

When we are old...

When we are old and these rejoicing veins
Are frosty channels to a muted stream,
And out of all our burning their remains
No feeblest spark to fire us, even in dream,
This be our solace: that it was not said
When we were young and warm and in our prime,
Upon our couch we lay as lie the dead,
Sleeping away the unreturning time.
O sweet, O heavy-lidded, O my love,
When morning strikes her spear upon the land,
And we must rise and arm us and reprove
The insolent daylight with a steady hand,
Be not discountenanced if the knowing know
We rose from rapture but an hour ago.

– Edna St. Vincent Millay

Love is not all…

Love is not all: it is not meat nor drink
Nor slumber nor a roof against the rain;
Nor yet a floating spar to men that sink
And rise and sink and rise and sink again;
Love cannot fill the thickened lung with breath,
Nor clean the blood, nor set the fractured bone;
Yet many a man is making friends with death
Even as I speak, for lack of love alone.
It well may be that in a difficult hour,
Pinned down by pain and moaning for release,
Or nagged by want past resolution's power,
I might be driven to sell your love for peace,
Or trade the memory of this night for food.
It well may be. I do not think I would.

– Edna St. Vincent Millay

When I too long have looked upon your face...

When I too long have looked upon your face,
Wherein for me a brightness unobscured
Save by the mists of brightness has its place,
And terrible beauty not to be endured,
I turn away reluctant from your light,
And stand irresolute, a mind undone,
A silly, dazzled thing deprived of sight
From having looked too long upon the sun.
Then is my daily life a narrow room
In which a little while, uncertainly,
Surrounded by impenetrable gloom,
Among familiar things grown strange to me
Making my way, I pause, and feel, and hark,
Till I become accustomed to the dark.

– Edna St. Vincent Millay

LOVE'S EPITAPH

A broken link in life's familiar chain,
A story ended, though the words remain.
Though time may smooth the edges, dull the smart,
The memory lives forever in the heart.

– Anon.

INDEX OF POETS

Akers Allen, Elizabeth	133
Apollinaire, Guillaume	161
Arnold, Matthew	119
Arvers, Félix	89
Austin, Alfred	135
Barrett Browning, Elizabeth	87
Baudelaire, Charles	104
Blake, William	49
Bradstreet, Anne	38
Breton, Nicholas	17
Bridges, Robert Seymour	141
Brooke, Rupert	170
Browning, Robert	99
Burns, Robert	51
Byron, George Gordon	63
Campion, Thomas	28
Cazalis, Henri	136
Clare, John	73
Coleridge, Samuel Taylor	56
Dickinson, Emily	127
Drayton, Michael	21
Dryden, John	40
Eliot, George	101
Fletcher, John	32
Ford, Thomas	33
Foster, Stephen	120
Gibran, Khalil	162
Goethe, Johann Wolfgang von	46
Hardy, Thomas	138
Heine, Heinrich	79
Herbert, George	36
Herrick, Robert	34
Hood, Thomas	83
Housman, A. E.	153
Hugo, Victor	86
Johnson, Samuel	42

INDEX OF POETS

Jonson, Ben	29
Keats, John	75
Kingsley, Charles	102
Lamartine, Alphonse de	66
Lovelace, Richard	39
McNally, Leonard	48
Marlowe, Christopher	26
Moore, Thomas	62
Morris, William	134
Nesbitt, Edith	152
Opie, Amelia	53
Poe, Edgar Allan	96
Rellstab, Ludwig	85
Ronsard, Pierre de	15
Rossetti, Christina	122
Schober, Franz von	78
Shakespeare, William	22
Shelley, Percy Bysshe	71
Sidney, Sir Philip	20
Somervell, Sir Arthur	156
Southey, Robert	61
Spenser, Edmund	18
St. Vincent Millay, Edna	172
Suckling, Sir John	37
Teasdale, Sara	165
Tennyson, Alfred	90
Verlaine, Paul	140
Wheeler Wilcox, Ella	145
Wilbye, John	31
Wilde, Oscar	151
Wilmot, John	41
Yeats, William Butler	157

INDEX OF TITLES AND FIRST LINES

A charm invests a face…	127
A Dream Within a Dream	96
A Farewell	102
A Hemisphere In Your Hair	109
A Perfect Whole	114
A Red, Red Rose	51
A Tragedy	152
After Love	169
Alone	167
Amaryllis	28
At Last	133
Annabel Lee	97
Beautiful Dreamer	120
Beauty and Beauty	171
Birds in the high hall garden…	92
Break, break, break…	90
Bright Star	75
By the Brook in Springtime	78
Come into the garden, Maud…	93
Come, my Celia, let us prove…	29
Down by the Salley Gardens	159
Drink to me only with thine eyes…	30
Echo	126
Evening Ode	42
Fair and True	17
First Love	73
Florentine Serenade	136
For each ecstatic instant…	129
Go not, happy day…	91
Go, Valentine	61
Hidden Flame	40
How do I love thee? Let me count the ways	88
How Can I Forget?	74
Hymn	113
I am not yours…	166
I Love You	150

INDEX OF TITLES AND FIRST LINES

I loved you first…	123
I prithee send me back my heart…	37
I Shall Not Care	168
I think I should have loved you presently…	172
I Will Not Let Thee Go	143
Ice and Fire	18
If thou must love me, let it be for nought…	87
If you were coming in the fall…	132
Invitation to a Journey	107
Jeanie with the Light Brown Hair	121
Let me not to the marriage of true minds…	23
Let These Be Your Desires	164
Life in a Love	100
Longing	119
Lorelei	82
Love (Rupert Brooke)	170
Love (Samuel Taylor Coleridge)	57
Love bade me welcome	36
Love's Coming	146
Love's Epitaph	177
Love's Language	148
Love's Philosophy	72
Love's Trinity	135
Love and Life	41
Love Is Enough	134
Love is not all…	174
Love not me for comely grace…	31
Love One Another	162
My delight and thy delight…	141
My Familiar Dream	140
My love is as a fever, longing still…	25
My mistress' eyes are nothing like the sun…	24
My Pretty Rose Tree	50
My soul conceals a secret…	89
My true love hath my heart…	20
Never give all the heart…	160

INDEX OF TITLES AND FIRST LINES

Neutral Tones	138
Now	99
Ode to Cassandra	15
Of Love	163
Oh, when I was in love with you...	154
One day I wrote her name...	19
One night as I lay with a wanton hussy...	112
Remember	122
Ruth	84
Secret Love	53
Serenade	85
Shall I compare thee to a summer's day?	22
She is far from the land...	62
She walks in beauty...	64
Silent Worship	156
Since there's no help...	21
So sweet love seemed that April morn...	142
So we'll go no more a-roving...	63
Solitude	66
Somewhere or other there must surely be...	125
Song to Celia — I	29
Song to Celia — II	30
Sonnet for Helen	16
Sweet Disorder	35
Sweet evenings come and go, love...	101
Summer	44
Take, oh, take those lips away...	32
Tell me not, Sweet...	39
That I did always love...	128
The Antidote	137
The Balcony	116
The Cloths of Heaven	158
The Coveted Jewels	80
The First Day	124
The Fountain	105

INDEX OF TITLES AND FIRST LINES

The Garden of Love	49
The Journey	86
The Kiss	165
The Lake	68
The Lass of Richmond Hill	48
The Lotus Flower	79
The Lovers' Death	118
The Lovers' Wine	117
The Lotus Flower	79
The Mirabeau Bridge	161
The Parting Kiss	52
The Passionate Shepherd to his Love	26
The Poison	111
The Portrait	115
The Presence of Love	56
The Voice	139
The Winter's Walk	43
There is a lady sweet and kind…	33
Time of Roses	83
To a Passer-By	104
To Fanny Brawne	76
To Jane	71
To My Dear and Loving Husband	38
To Stella	45
To Virgins, to make much of Time	34
Unrequited Love	81
Welcome and Farewell	47
When I too long have looked upon your face…	175
When I was one-and-twenty…	155
When the lad for longing sighs…	153
When we are old…	173
When we two parted…	65
When you are old and grey	157
Wild nights - Wild nights!…	131
When Love Is Lost	145
Who Ever Loved, That Loved Not at First Sight?	27

INDEX OF TITLES AND FIRST LINES

Would You Were Here!	46
You Will Forget Me	147
You left me, sweet, two legacie…s	130
You say you love, but with a voice…	77
Young and Old	103

www.ingramcontent.com/pod-product-compliance
Lightning Source LLC
Chambersburg PA
CBHW060658100426
42735CB00040B/3027